J. Anne Helgren

Himalayan Cats

Everything about Acquisition, Care, Nutrition, Behavior, Health Care, and Breeding

With 46 Color Photographs

Illustrations by David Wenzel

BARRON'S

Dedication

To Libby Basore and Rebecca Rose Basore with love and gratitude for lifelong support, and to Mr. Bill always.

—J. Anne Helgren
1995

© Copyright 1996 by Barron's Educational Series, Inc.

All inquiries should be addressed to:
Barron's Educational Series, Inc.
250 Wireless Boulevard
Hauppauge, NY 11788

International Standard Book No. 0-8120-9242-2

Library of Congress Catalog Card No. 95-41069

Library of Congress Cataloging-in-Publication Data
Helgren, J. Anne.
    Himalayan cats : everything about acquisition, care, nutrition, behavior, health care, and breeding / J. Anne Helgren ; illustrations by David Wenzel.
        p.   cm. — (A Complete pet owner's manual)
    Includes bibliographical references (p.   ) and index.
    ISBN 0-8120-9242-2
    1. Himalayan cat. I. Title. II. Series.
SF449.H55H45   1996
636.8'3—dc20   95-41069
                                    CIP

Printed in Hong Kong

6789   9955   987654

About the Author

J. Anne Helgren is a contributing editor and writes the featured "Breed of the Month" column for *Cats Magazine*. She is a professional member of the Cat Writers' Association and has written dozens of articles on cats for national and regional magazines and newspapers. She is the author *Abyssinian Cats*, a Barron's Pet Owner's Manual. Helgren has a lifetime of experience with the feline species and has conducted extensive research on cat-related topics, including interviews with breeders, judges, fanciers, and veterinarians. She lives near Sacramento, California, with her husband, Bill, and four feline friends.

Photo Credits
Chanan: front cover, pages 9, 16 top, 20, 25, 28, 37, 64 top, 68, 77; Donna J. Coss: back cover, inside back cover, pages 36, 53, 69, 89; Susan Green: pages 16 bottom, 24, 52 top and bottom, 57 bottom, 61; J. Anne Helgren: page 41; Don Himsel: pages 12, 56, 93 top and bottom; Mark McCullough: inside front cover, pages 4, 8 top and bottom, 17, 29, 45, 57 top, 60 top, 64 bottom, 65, 72, 76, 81; Bob Schwartz: pages 21, 32, 33, 41, 44, 48, 60 bottom, 84, 99.

Important Note

When you handle cats, you may sometimes get scratched or bitten. If this happens, have a doctor treat the injuries immediately.

Make sure your cat receives all the necessary shots and dewormings, otherwise serious danger to the animal and to human health may arise. A few diseases and parasites can be communicated to humans. If your cat shows any signs of illness, you should definitely consult a veterinarian. If you are worried about your own health, see your doctor and tell him or her that you have cats.

Some people have allergic reactions to cats. If you think you might be allergic, see your doctor before you get a cat.

It is possible for a cat to cause damage to someone else's property and even to cause accidents. For your own protection you should make sure your insurance covers such eventualities, and you should definitely have liability insurance.

Contents

Preface 5

What Is a Himalayan? 6
Origin of the Himalayan 6
The Breed Standard 8
Temperament 10

Buying a Himalayan 13
Before You Buy 13
Which Himalayan Is Right for
  You? 14
Price 15
Choosing a Kitten 15
The Sales Contract 16
Choosing a Breeder 17

Understanding Himalayan Cats 20
Social Behavior 20
Play 22
Cat Language 22
Vocal Communication 23
Body Language 24
Hunting and Predation 25
How Cats Hunt 25
Covering Their Tracks 26

Acclimation and Daily Life 27
Preparing for Arrival 27
Finding a Veterinarian 30
Bringing Home Baby 31
Handling Your Himalayan 31
Kittens and Kids 32
The Adjustment Period 33
Teaching Your Himalayan 33
Scratching Problems 33
Declawing 34
Dealing with Cat Hair 35
Litter Box Problems 36
Spaying and Neutering 38
Spending Time with Your
  Himalayan 38
Adding a Second Cat 39

Environmental Hazards 40
Outdoor Hazards 40
HOW-TO: Cat-Proofing Your
  Home 42
Indoor Hazards 44

Grooming Your Himalayan 45
Grooming Products 45
Nail Care 47
Eyes and Ears 47
Teeth 48
Coat Care 49
HOW-TO: Bathing Your
  Himalayan 50
The Grooming Session 52

Nutrition and Feeding 55
Dietary Needs 55
Stages of Life 58
Types of Cat Foods 58
Pet Food Labels 59
Treats 62
Catnip 62

Health Care and Diseases 63
Serious Symptoms 63
Vaccinations 63
Diseases and Illnesses 65
Respiratory Ailments 67
Lower Urinary Tract Disease 68
Hairballs 68
Eye Ailments 69
HOW-TO: Caring for Your Sick
  Himalayan 70
Ear Problems 72
Parasites 72
Skin Problems 74
Toxoplasmosis 74
Abscesses 75
Obesity 75
The Senior Himalayan 75
Euthanasia 76

Seal Lynxpoint Himalayan. Lynxpoint Himalayans must have the classic tabby "M" marking on the forehead.

Feline First Aid 77
HOW-TO: Cardiopulmonary
    Resuscitation—CPR 78

Sexual Behavior 85
The Queen's Heat 85
The Tom's Rut 86
Mating 86

Breeding Your Himalayan 88
Before Breeding Your Himalayan 88
Feline Genetics 88
The Pointed Coat Pattern 90
Coat Colors 90
Finding a Queen 91
Finding a Stud 91
The Stud Fee 92
Pregnancy 92

The Birth 93
Pregnancy Problems 95
Kitten Care 95

Showing Your Himalayan 96
Cat Organizations 96
The First Cat Shows 96
Today's Shows 97
How a Cat Show Works 97
Showing Your Himalayan 98
Grooming the Show
    Himalayan 99
Attending the Show 99

**Useful Addresses and
    Literature 101**

Index 103

Preface

Luxuriously furred felines have long fascinated cat lovers around the globe. While human hair fashions come and go, Himalayans and their Persian cousins have enjoyed a long reign within the cat fancy—a popularity that shows no signs of waning. Their beautiful coats, pleasing personalities, and feline magnetism make them one of the most popular breeds to grace the cat fancy today. And why shouldn't Himalayans be popular? They are beautiful, sweet, lovable, and best of all, they're *cats*, with all the mystery and charm that have fascinated humankind for thousands of years.

Over the millennia, humans and cats have been allies, friends, companions—and bitter enemies, depending upon the period and the emotional climate. Cats have been worshiped as gods and persecuted as demons. Cats have been both loved and loathed—but rarely *ignored*.

Perhaps our examination of the mysterious nature of felines is akin to our search for meaning in our lives. Those luminous eyes seem to reflect a higher knowledge that they are not yet prepared to share with us mere humans. Maybe someday they'll share their wisdom. When they deem us ready.

Acknowledgments

The author would like to thank Grace Freedson and Mary Falcon (Barron's Educational Series, Inc.) and Roy and Tracey Copeland (*CATS* Magazine), for their help and guidance; photographer Mark McCullough (Through The Cat's Eye Studio) and photographer Cynthia Forde DeBois (and her assistant, Feather) for the photographs; and Laura Lane and Arnold Schwartzakatz for patiently posing. The author would also like to thank Robin Montgomery for her invaluable support and friendship; Sue Campbell, Rhonda Darnell, Arlene Evans, Bill Helgren, John Lehman, Betty Roby, and Larry and Zil Snyder for their help, encouragement, and advice; Louise Feaver Crawford, Cleo Kocol, Susan Scheibel, and Suzanne Suzuki for their valued friendship and support (and for patiently listening to all of my cat stories), and, finally, Pooka for the Siamese point of view.

What Is a Himalayan?

Origin of the Himalayan

Cats are relative newcomers to domestication, and have always accepted humankind's domination with certain reservations. Most of our modern domestic animals (sheep, pigs, and goats, to name a few) were domesticated long before the feline. Canines were domesticated an estimated 20,000 years ago, about 16,000 years before cats began their alliance with humans.

Domestic cats descended from the African wild cat *Felis silvestris libyca.* This species has the same structure and number of chromosomes as the domestic cat; the two species can interbreed and produce fertile offspring. Many of the cat remains mummified by the cat cult that existed 4,000 years ago in Egypt are *Felis libyca.*

Some experts believe that cats domesticated humankind, not the other way around. When humans evolved from the hunter-gatherer existence to an agrarian culture,

Felis libyca, *the progenitor of all domestic breeds.*

cats learned that humans were useful for providing a reliable food source—namely the rodents attracted to the stored grain. Humans soon learned that felines were useful, too, in their way. Cats became invaluable colleagues in controlling rodent populations. Somewhere along the way, humans discovered cats were amiable comrades, too, and vice versa. It's worked out quite well all the way around.

Cats became household companions to the Egyptians at least 4,000 years ago. Egyptian artists of that period depicted cats on many ornaments, statues, bas-reliefs, and paintings. Like humans, cats were often mummified. Archaeologists found thousands of such cats buried with mummified mice and shrews preserved to sustain the cats on their journey to the afterlife.

How cats went from mousetraps to messengers of the gods (in the eyes of the ancient Egyptians, anyway), is uncertain. The cat worshippers apparently believed the cat's ability to see at night was magical. Because cats' eyes reflect the sun, the Egyptians believed cats had the power to protect humans from darkness and death. The Egyptian word for cat is *Mau,* which means "to see."

However, before you get the impression that ancient Egyptians were cat lovers like today's fanciers, consider the cult's darker side. Cat remains indicate that many of the mummified cats died at a young age. Their necks had been broken, suggesting that the cult also may have indulged in ritual feline sacrifice.

From Egypt, travelers transported cats to Europe, the Orient, and Japan.

Many cultures, like those of the Japanese and Chinese, came to appreciate felines for their beauty, wisdom, and usefulness. In Thailand (formerly Siam), the domestic cat breed we know as the Siamese developed. The Siamese is one of two breeds used in the creation of the Himalayan.

Evidence that these beautiful pointed pattern cats existed as long ago as 1350 A.D can be found in a manuscript called The *Cat-Book Poems*, written in the Siamese city of Ayudha. The Thai people greatly valued these cats and kept them in their temples and palaces to guard the documents and valuables. As the story goes, these sacred Siamese temple cats, charged with guarding the temples' treasures, stared at the valuables with such intensity that their eyes became crossed.

Not all cultures appreciated cats, however. The religious sects of fourteenth century Europe shunned, persecuted, and killed cats for a supposed link with the devil. Because of the decimated cat populations, rodents flourished, and with them so did the bubonic plague, which from 1347 to 1351 A.D. killed 75 million people—approximately one half of the population of Asia, Europe, Africa, and Egypt. Even after the great plague ended, outbreaks continued for many years. Domestic cats, unsung crusaders in the war against disease, played a major role in reducing those outbreaks by ridding towns and villages of rodents. So if anyone tells you cats are useless, remind them of the Black Death!

With the advent of sailing ships, domestic cats spread throughout the world, arriving in America with the Pilgrims, or perhaps centuries earlier with the Vikings. Cats can certainly be considered part of our national heritage.

Researchers are not sure where the Persian (the other breed in the Himalayan equation) originated. They think the gene for long hair appeared as a spontaneous mutation in the domestic cat population in the mountainous areas of Iran, then called Persia, for which the Persian cat was named.

In the sixteenth century, the Romans and Phoenicians transported Persian cats to continental Europe and eventually to Britain. Persian cats quickly became popular for their long coats and sweet temperaments, and were one of the first breeds exhibited in early cat shows. In the early 1900s, the Governing Council of the Cat Fancy (GCCF) in Britain decided that all longhaired cats—Persians, Angoras, and longhaired Russians—would be grouped under the name *longhair*, with each color constituting a separate breed. This policy continues today.

In 1924, a Swedish geneticist made the first attempt at a deliberate crossing between a Siamese and a longhaired cat. Six years later, two Harvard medical employees crossed a Siamese female with a black Persian male, not to create a new breed, but to study genetic color inheritance. A litter of black, shorthaired kittens resulted. They then bred a black Persian female with a Siamese male, with the same outcome.

However, by crossing a female from the second litter with a male from the first, they produced Debutante, the first pointed pattern longhair, which had the Siamese body type like today's Balinese breed. (The Himalayan should not be confused with the Balinese or Javanese; these longhaired pointed breeds have the Oriental body type of the Siamese rather than the cobby [see page 9] type of the Persian.) At this point, the Harvard employees ended their experiment, but breeders in England took up the torch and began their own Persian/Siamese crosses. These breeders hoped to produce a cat with

The Himalayan's color pattern comes from its Siamese ancestors.

The Himalayan body mirrors the Persian's cobby design, rather than the Siamese's foreign type.

the Siamese pointed pattern and the popular Persian hair and body type.

During the World War II years, interest in the breeding program waned. But, in 1950, American breeder Marguerita Goforth succeeded in creating an entirely new longhaired breed, one with the Siamese's beautiful coat color and pattern and the Persian's popular body type. Five years later, the Governing Council of the Cat Fancy recognized the Himalayan under the name *Colorpoint Longhair.* The American Cat Fanciers' Association (ACFA) and the Cat Fanciers' Association (CFA) recognized the breed under the name *Himalayan* in 1957. The breed was so named for the Himalayan pointed pattern found in other animals such as the Himalayan rabbit. By 1961, all major U.S. cat associations recognized the Himalayan.

Today, the Himalayan is recognized as a separate breed by the American Association of Cat Enthusiasts (AACE), the American Cat Fanciers' Association (ACFA), the Cat Fanciers' Federation (CFF), the National Cat Fanciers' Association (NCFA), and The International Cat Association (TICA). The American Cat Association (ACA) and the Cat Fanciers' Association (CFA) recognize the Himalayan as a color division of the Persian, and refer to the breed as the Pointed Pattern Persian. Cats who carry the colorpoint gene but look like Persians are called Colorpoint Carriers and are given a separate identification number. In combining the breeds, CFA made Himalayan/Persian hybrids eligible for championship competition. The NCFA (and others) disagree with this policy, and originally formed to promote the Himalayan as a separate, distinct breed.

The Breed Standard

The Himalayan's shape is often described as "a shoe box with legs."

The cat fancy term for this body type is *cobby*. A purebred breed's standard is a guideline describing the characteristics that make a supreme example of the breed. Each characteristic is assigned a number of points. A perfect cat would earn 100 points, but few can attain such a score.

A committee of judges, breeders, and/or fanciers draft and update the standard as necessary. The standards and points awarded to each characteristic varies from one cat association to another.

The current show trend is toward a more extreme facial type. This troubles some fanciers, who feel the extreme face is harmful to the breed. Reported difficulties include breathing distress, malocclusions, dermatitis in the facial folds, and birthing difficulties because of the size of the kittens' heads.

Keep in mind that the standard is an ideal for which to strive. A Himalayan that would earn no ribbons in the show ring will still make a fine companion. The following is a general standard and will vary, depending upon the association. The point range shows the lowest and highest assigned by the associations. The objections reduce the point score that the judge awards.

General: The Himalayan should resemble the Persian in type, conformation, coat length, and texture. The pointed Himalayan has the Siamese's eye color, coat color, and pattern. The nonpointed Himalayan has the Persian's eye color, coat color, and pattern. Any similarity in body type to the Siamese is undesirable.

Head: 20 to 30 points. Round and massive with great breadth of skull. Chin well developed. Round face with round underlying bone structure. Jaws broad and powerful, cheeks full and prominent. Nose snub, as broad as it is long. A distinct skull indentation between the eyes divides the two planes of the skull, called a break. The top of the nose leather should be no higher than the middle of the eye. The general appearance of the face should be open and pleasant. *Objection*: Long, narrow head, long nose, thin muzzle, overshot or undershot jaw, bite deformity.

Ears: 5 to 7 points. Small, round-tipped, tilting forward, set wide apart and low on the head, fitting into, and without distorting, the head's roundness. *Objection*: Large, pointed, set too close.

Eyes: 8 to 10 points. Large, round, and full. Set wide apart, giving a sweet expression to the face. Color blue; brilliant, intense color preferred. *Objection*: Small, too close together, Oriental or slanted, pale color, apparent obstruction of the tear drainage ducts.

Body: 15 to 30 points. Cobby in type—low on the legs, deep in the chest, equally massive across the shoulders and rump. Back short and level. Neck short and powerful. Midsection firm and well-rounded.

Bluepoint Himalayan. The color blue in cat fancy terms actually appears as gray. Blue is a genetic dilute of seal.

Notice the difference in skull structure between the Siamese and the Himalayan.

Heavily boned with good muscle tone. Medium to large in size. Quality and proportion the determining consideration.

Legs and Feet: 8 to 10 points. Legs should be short, thick, and heavily boned. Musculature firm and well-developed. Feet are large, round, and firm with toes close together. Five toes in front, four behind. *Objection*: Light boning, long or bowed legs, small or oval feet.

Tail: 5 to 7 points. Short, straight, in proportion to the body. *Objection*: Long tail.

Coat: 10 to 15 points. Long, thick, soft, silky, glossy, fine texture, full of life, standing off from the body. Long all over the body, including the shoulders. Ruff immense and continues in a deep frill between the front legs. Seasonal variations of the coat shall be recognized.

Color and Pattern: 15 to 20 points. The mask, ears, legs, and tail should be clearly defined in darker shade but should merge gently into the body color on legs. The body color should be a pastel version of the point color, shading to a paler shade on the chest and belly (this change is less apparent on the lighter colors). Slight spotting on stomach not penalized on queens. Allowance should be made for body darkening in older cats, and for lighter or incomplete markings in kittens and young cats. *Objection*: Mismatched points and poor contrast between body and point color. Light hairs in points, white toes or patches of white in points. Bars or tabby markings on colors other than Lynx Points.

Condition and Balance: 10 to 20 points. Firm in the flesh but not fat, well-balanced physically and temperamentally, gentle and amenable to handling. Medium to large in size. Heavily boned, short-coupled, broad through the chest and rump with short, sturdy legs, giving the impression of robust power.

Disqualify/Withhold Wins: Any other color eyes than blue in pointeds. Crossed eyes. Kinked tail or any tail abnormality. Lack of nose break. White toes or feet, locket or button. Incorrect number of toes. Apparent weakness in hindquarters. Deformity of skull and/or mouth. Severe malocclusion. Aggressively unfriendly disposition. Poor condition.

Temperament

Himmies, as Himalayans are affectionately called, are sweet, gentle, alert, and playful—the perfect indoor cat companion. On the cat activity level "Richter scale," (with, perhaps, the Abyssinian as the active "ten" and the Persian as the serene "one"), the Himalayan is a moderate "three"— gentle, calm, and sweet, but with a playful side as well. Far from aloof, Himalayans are as loving and devoted as any cat lover could want. Extremely affectionate and loyal to their chosen humans, they crave attention, and love to be petted, groomed, and fussed over. When neglected, they pine.

Your Himalayan friend loves to sit in your lap (if the temperature is not too warm), cuddle in bed with you at night, and follow you from room to room to keep an eye on what you're doing. Your cat wants to make sure your activities meet with Himalayan approval.

Because of the Siamese influence, Himalayans are in general livelier than their Persian counterparts. Like the Siamese, Himalayans love to play "fetch" and will bring toys back to you to toss. A scrap of crumpled paper or a feather will entertain them as well as the most expensive cat toy. A Himalayan, as any Himmie fancier will tell you, is the perfect companion with which to share your home and life.

Cats are judged according to how well they conform to the breed standard. The standard awards a number of points to certain traits, equaling a total of 100 points:

CFA Point Score

Head (including size and shape of eyes, ear shape and set	*30*
Type including shape, size, bone, and length of tail	*20*
Coat	*10*
Balance	*5*
Refinement	*5*
Color	*20*
Eye Color	*10*
Total	*100*

Sealpoint Himalayan. The Himalayan's most outstanding feature is its luxurious fur, which can reach six to eight inches in length.

Buying a Himalayan

Before You Buy

As with all important decisions, buying a Himalayan requires careful consideration. Grooming is a major factor. A Himalayan must be groomed regularly to keep her fur from developing mats and snarls. If you cannot devote five minutes a day to your cat's grooming, and don't have the time and energy to provide a once-a-month bathing and thorough grooming session, you'd do better to select a short-haired breed. The Exotic Shorthair, for example, has the Himalayan's body style and personality, but has a short, easy-to-care-for coat.

I firmly feel that all cats should be kept indoors when not closely supervised by their human companions, for reasons that will be explored in later chapters. The Himalayan, with her accepting temperament and long fur, is particularly suited to the indoors. If keeping a cat indoors is not an option, a different kind of pet might be a better choice.

Be sure you have the time for a cat. Cats in general are less dependent than dogs, but it's a myth that cats require no care. Himalayans are people-oriented and require from you a commitment of time, as do all cats.

Be sure you're financially able to have a Himalayan. The costs can add up when you consider cat food, litter, veterinary care, medications, vaccinations, spaying and neutering, toys, and care when you are absent.

Finally, be sure you are emotionally suited to share your life with a Himalayan. Cats, like all living creatures, will occasionally cause you inconvenience. Can you forgive your cat for scratching the furniture, toppling a vase, or coughing up a hairball on your carpet? Can you accept these annoyances without losing your temper and mistreating your cat?

Will you still love your Himalayan when she grows up? Kittenhood is the shortest period of a cat's life and will soon be over. If you are not looking forward to your cat's adult years, please don't buy a Himalayan or any kind of cat.

Housing Considerations

If you are renting, get written permission from the landlord before bringing a cat home. Don't try to sneak the cat into the apartment and hope the landlord doesn't find out. Too many cats (and dogs, too) end up in shelters that way.

The landlord may have you sign a liability agreement, and may ask for an additional pet damage deposit. This is not unreasonable. Be sure the agreement doesn't state that the landlord has the right to forbid you from owning a cat at a later time.

Other Pets

A Himalayan, with her mellow personality, can adapt well to cats, dogs, and other animals once she accepts them as family members. Himalayans are natural predators; provide protection for small pets such as hamsters, rats, mice, and birds. Covering the aquarium will keep your cat from going fishing.

However, a more active cat breed may annoy a Himalayan, so it's a

In the male, the space between the anus and the genital opening is greater than in the female. The female's genital opening looks like a small slit, whereas the male's sexual orifice is round.

good idea to match your cat companions' activity levels. For example, the Himalayan would be a good companion for a Persian, Angora, Exotic Shorthair, Birman, Ragdoll, or Maine Coon. The Himalayan might not do as well with an Abyssinian, Cornish Rex, Ocicat, or Bengal. These breeds tend to dominate the easy-going and less active Himalayan.

If You Travel

Consider who will look after your cat while you're traveling. It's best if a trusted friend or relative can stay at your house while you're gone, so the cat can remain in a familiar environment. Or have a relative or friend drop in a few times a day to feed and check on the cat.

Another option is a bonded cat-sitting service. These services provide in-home feeding and care for your cat while you're away. Ask for references and call the Better Business Bureau to check for complaints before committing.

Boarding services are also available, and some provide luxurious accommodations. Check out these facilities carefully. You would be wise not to use a boarding service that doesn't require proof of vaccination for its boarders.

Which Himalayan Is Right for You?

Pet quality Himalayans are the most affordable. They are purebred and fully registerable, but in the breeder's estimation they will not be suitable for competition in the cat shows because of cosmetic flaws of coat, conformation, or color. Pet quality doesn't mean the cats are not healthy or won't make fine companions.

Breeder quality Himalayans have good potential for producing quality offspring. A Himalayan breeder may sell breeder quality cats for slightly less than show quality cats.

Show quality Himalayans are assessed by the breeder to be outstanding examples of the breed, and they should do well in competition. Show quality cats are the most expensive. Some breeders also sell *top show* Himalayans. This means the breeder believes the cats can make finals consistently after they have achieved grand champion status and are good enough to compete for high regional or national awards. If you are interested in a show quality Himalayan, wait until the kitten is at least six months old to buy her. The kitten's show prospects can be judged more easily if you wait until the kitten is out of the lanky "teenager" period.

My tip: If you want a Himalayan for a companion and you have little or no interest in showing, I recommend pet quality. A pet quality Himalayan will make as good a companion as the finest grand champion, and will cost considerably less.

Price

Price varies greatly depending on area, availability, color, gender, blood-lines, and show prospects. Read the breed standard (see page 9), talk to breeders, and take in a few cat shows before starting the selection process so you'll know what you're looking for. It's rare, but some disreputable people represent their cats as show quality when they know their cats are not worthy of that classification. On the other hand, if a breeder or dealer is selling Himalayans for much less than average, be wary. Discounted Himalayans are risky business and may have genetic defects, health concerns, or behavior problems. It pays to be an informed consumer.

Although Himalayans lean toward a certain personality type, each kitten is an individual. Some kittens are outgoing and bold, and others prefer to watch from the sidelines.

Choosing a Kitten

Look for a kitten that's healthy, happy, and alert. A healthy kitten is curious and playful. Her fur is clean, soft, fluffy, and glossy, never rough. Look at the roots of the fur. If you see tiny black particles clinging to the hairs, this means trouble (see Fleas, page 73).

A healthy kitten's eyes are bright and clear and do not run. The face shouldn't have tear stains. Her nose should be damp and cool to the touch. The kitten should not sneeze or wheeze, and the nose shouldn't run. This could be a sign of respiratory problems.

The kitten's ears should be clean and free of dark colored wax. The kitten shouldn't shake her head or scratch at her ears. That's an indication of infection or ear mites. The anus should be free of fecal matter or evidence of diarrhea.

Gently pry open the kitten's mouth. A healthy kitten's gums and mouth are pink with no sign of inflammation. The teeth are clean and white.

A 12-week-old kitten should have her first and second shots (see immuniza-tion schedule on page 65). Her fecal exam should show her to be free of parasites. Ask for a copy of her veteri-nary records when you buy the kitten.

A kitten's temperament is equally important. Observe the litter for a few minutes. Tempt the kittens with a cat toy and see how they react. You'll notice some kittens are bold, while others prefer to hang back and check out the action from a safe distance. Look for a kitten that seems curious, friendly, intelligent, and used to han-dling. Don't choose a kitten that cow-ers from your hand, runs away in terror, hisses, snarls, or struggles wildly. Avoid kittens that appear overly passive or unresponsive. This could be a sign of health problems as well as temperament concerns.

Cats are individuals; they behave according to their unique natures. In any given litter, you'll notice a range of behavior. However (there's always a however), one reason for buying a purebred is that she follows the breed's standard. You can be sure the kitten will exhibit some of the Himalayan behaviors.

Himalayan kittens. When choosing a kitten, select one that is curious, friendly, intelligent, and seems used to handling.

My tip: If all the kittens seem unaccustomed to human contact (provided they are over six weeks old), find another breeder. Kittens with little early human contact are less likely to form strong, trusting bonds with their humans.

The Sales Contract

Most breeders have conditions under which they sell their cats. Read the contract carefully. If you have questions or concerns about the conditions, ask the breeder for clarification. If you think the conditions are unreasonable or too restrictive, buy from another breeder. Once you sign the contract, you are legally and morally obliged to honor it.

Breeder contracts vary. Common issues addressed include declawing, breeding, spaying and neutering, and the cat's care, housing, diet, and medical treatment. Some contracts require you to keep the cat indoors, and to give the breeder an opportunity to buy the cat back if you can no longer keep it. Many contracts prohibit the cat from being sold or given to pet shops, shelters, or research laboratories.

If the kitten is pet quality and not being sold for breeding purposes, the contract will usually require that you

Redpoint Himalayans are also called Flamepoints, depending upon the cat association.

16

Exotic Shorthair. If the grooming responsibility of a Himalayan seems too great, the Exotic Shorthair is an excellent alternative. This breed has the body style and temperament of the Himalayan, but has a short, easy-to-care-for coat.

not breed the cat, and that she be altered when she's old enough. It's also a common practice for the breeder to withhold the cat's papers until you provide proof of alteration.

Choosing a Breeder

The best way to ensure the quality of the Himalayan you purchase is to buy it directly from the breeder. If you choose to buy through a pet shop, ask for verification that the shop obtained the cat from a reputable breeder. Avoid buying a Himalayan from a private party or a newspaper ad. "Backyard breeders" (people who breed only for profit and often have substandard stock), usually sell their cats through newspaper ads and flyers.

Finding a Himalayan breeder is easy. Just pick up a copy of one of the magazines listed on pages 101–102 and check the breeder listings. If the breeder has no Himalayans available,

he or she may recommend another breeder who does. Breeders often associate with one another. Or ask the breeder to inform you when kittens are available. Sometimes you can put down a deposit. If at all possible, see the kitten personally before agreeing to buy him.

Cat magazines also have listings of upcoming cat shows. Attending a cat show is a great way to meet breeders and see their cats. Breeders who produce cats that meet the breed standard will likely also show their cats. You *usually* will not find breeders at cat shows who produce poor quality cats. At such shows their cats are subject to scrutiny by experienced judges, exhibitors, and breeders who can quickly spot a bad apple in their bunch.

Contact a cat association-affiliated Himalayan or Persian breed society; such societies can provide member lists. These organizations usually have a written code of breeder ethics the members agree to uphold. The cat associations can provide club information and have lists of breeder members they can provide (see list on page 101).

Call breeders on weekday evenings, before 9 P.M., please! On weekends, breeders are often away at cat shows. In the initial conversation, ask questions and expect questions in return. Prepare a list before calling. A caring breeder will be willing to answer all questions. The breeder may also have material to send you, including photographs of his or her cats. If the breeder lives far away, ask to see photos. Call the cat association or society to which the breeder belongs to check credentials.

In many cases you'll have to wait before picking up a Himalayan. Responsible breeders do not release their kittens until they are at least 12 weeks old, and some hold onto their kittens for 16 weeks or longer. It's vital to a kitten's development that he

spend the first weeks of life with his mother, so don't begrudge the kitten the extra time.

Questions You Should Ask

First of all, ask how the kittens are raised. You want a kitten who has been raised "underfoot" in a loving home environment, rather than in an isolated cattery with little human contact. Also ask if you can see both of the parents, or only the mother. By seeing the parents, you'll have a better idea of the adult appearance and temperament of the offspring.

Ask the breeder to provide names and phone numbers of people with whom he or she has previously placed cats. Then ask these Himalayan owners about their experiences with the breeder. Of course, a breeder is likely to provide only the phone numbers of those who have had positive experiences.

Ask whether a veterinarian examined the kittens, what vaccinations have been given, and if the kittens have been tested for Feline Leukemia (FeLV). Ask if the breeder guarantees the kitten against genetic or health problems.

Finally, ask in what cat association(s) the breeder's cats are registered. This is important if you decide to show the cat, because each cat association has different show standards and rules regarding the Himalayan breed.

Visiting the Cattery

Whenever possible, choose a breeder whose cattery you can visit, because that will enable you to see how the kittens have been raised. Most breeders operate their catteries out of their homes.

When visiting the cattery, let your eyes and nose be your guide—does the place smell clean, or does it reek of urine and feces? Does the cattery look tidy and well cared for? Are the

Visiting the cattery will give you a good idea of how the kittens have been raised.

cats comfortable around people, or do they slink around and hide? Are toys, scratching posts, and other cat items in evidence, or do you get the impression the breeder views cats as just a moneymaking venture?

Regardless of whether you're buying a pet, breed, or show quality kitten, ask the breeder for an explanation of the traits that determine the classification. If the kitten is not suitable for show, ask the breeder why. If the breeder is truly familiar with the breed standard, he or she should be able to give a rundown of a kitten's qualities and imperfections. It is essential to be familiar with the standard before choosing a kitten. You'll then have a better understanding of the cat's traits and flaws.

Questions Your Breeder May Ask

A responsible breeder will also ask questions before selling a kitten. Some questions may seem rather personal, but try not to take offense. Caring breeders are attached to their cats, and want to make sure their special "kids" go to loving, trustworthy homes. In fact, a breeder who seems eager to sell to just anyone could be a bad risk. If the breeder isn't concerned about finding good homes for the kittens, how much care do you think he or she put into breeding the kittens in the first place?

Expect the breeder to ask questions about your lifestyle. For example, you may be asked whether you will be away from home a great deal, whether you have young children, what kind of housing you live in, and if you're willing to keep the cat indoors. The breeder may ask what you will feed the kitten, if you plan to declaw, and your views on spaying and neutering. The breeder may want to know what you would do if you couldn't keep the cat any longer, how much you know about the Himalayan breed, and whether you're aware of the substantial grooming commitment this breed requires.

Understanding Himalayan Cats

The feline is probably the least understood domestic animal species. In the 4,000 or so years cats have associated themselves with humans, they have been wrongly accused of any number of behaviors and attitudes from the totally absurd (being in league with the Devil) to the merely misinterpreted (being independent of their human companions). Felines often act in ways that can seem strange to us, but that's because we don't always understand the way cats think and communicate. By understanding feline behavior in general, you'll have a closer relationship with your Himalayan friend.

Cats are social animals. The mistaken idea that cats are solitary has haunted felines for years, possibly because cats are solitary hunters, and therefore humans have made the error of thinking cats don't seek their own kind for companionship as well.

Social Behavior

Cats are territorial by nature, and their society is structured in a dominance-controlled hierarchy governed by strict rules of conduct.

Males in a feline community fight to determine their order in the dominance hierarchy. When a new tom arrives in the territory, he must fight

Himalayan kittens. During the sixth week of life, the Himalayan's beautiful coat begins to grow.

the established toms to confirm his place in the social structure. Once he establishes his rank, he doesn't have to fight again unless challenged for his place or challenges a higher ranking tom's position. Males also fight over the chance to mate with female cats in heat (see Sexual Behavior, page 85). The top ranking tom cat controls the largest territory.

Female cats have the social hierarchy as well, but it's arranged more loosely. With each new litter, a queen increases her social status. A queen with kittens, regardless of prior social status, dramatically moves up the social ladder. Female cats will cooperate with each other more than will male cats, and will sometimes nurse and take care of each other's kittens.

While females hold less territory than the males, they defend it more fiercely, particularly if they have kittens to protect. Queens are loving, protective mothers, whereas tom cats pay little attention to kittens—their's or anybody else's—and may even try to kill them. Male lions exhibit the same behavior and will kill the cubs of other males to assure genetic survival.

When neutered or spayed, male and female cats quickly lose their place in the feline hierarchy, and cats who are altered before establishing their rank have no status in the social order. However, this is not a good excuse for failing to spay or neuter your cats.

Clubbing: This is a little-understood feline social behavior. Male and female cats gather at an appointed meeting ground and peacefully sit near one another, groom, and socialize. After a few hours of this amiable mingling, the cats go back home to their own territories. Occasionally, mating takes place at these gatherings, but these soirees have no obvious sexual significance. Biologists don't understand this behavior, but it obviously fulfills some important social need.

Because of their facial structure, some Himalayans may appear aloof and haughty. Nothing could be further from the truth. Himalayans make delightful, loving companions.

An indoor-only cat, alone all day and deprived of feline company, suffers from loneliness and may become depressed, as we do when we are kept from the company of our peers. While Himalayans get much of their social needs from their favorite humans, it's wise to provide your indoor cat with a feline companion.

Indoor cats do not lose their territorial instinct, but the territorial boundaries in multi-cat homes are usually small, and can vary depending upon the time of day. Favorite sleeping spots, cat furniture, the rug by the fire, or even a sunny spot by the window can be claimed by the dominant cat.

Members of an indoor-only clan usually arrange themselves into an amiable hierarchy, with one dominant cat in charge and all the rest of the cats sharing middle rank. Over time, the territorial boundaries often blur until the cats peacefully share the entire household domain. All cats need at least one spot to call their own, however, and overcrowding is as upsetting to cats as it is to humans.

Scapegoats: sometimes, particularly if overcrowded, one or two lower rank felines become scapegoats for the rest of the group and are universally abused by the community. Biologists believe this is a social "safety valve" that prevents the feline social structure from breaking down into chaos. (This analysis would seem to give us an interesting glimpse into human behavior as well.)

Play

Cats—kittens in particular—love to play. That's what make kittens so fun

The four body postures: friendly and curious (top left), submissive and uncertain (top right), frightened and defensive (bottom left), angry and aggressive (bottom).

to watch. Life is one long game, and it's hard to be melancholy while watching a Himalayan kitten roll about the floor with such abandonment. Play serves important functions as well, for kittens are learning important social and hunting skills while they wrestle with each other.

Early socialization is important. Cats who have been taken away from their mothers too early have problems later in life. Mother cats teach not only hunting skills but also social skills. (Poorly socialized cats, untutored in the survival skills, are usually poor hunters.) A cat's lack of social skills can affect his relationship with humans, too. For example, cats who lack proper upbringing can bite too hard when playing, because they didn't learn to "pull their punches" when they were kittens.

Cat Language

Cats use a variety of vocal, physical, and scent-marking signals to communicate their feelings and needs. Cats use scent marking in several ways. Rubbing is the most common form of this marking behavior. You'll notice this when your cat feels affectionate toward you, or around dinner time. The cat brushes up against you, rubbing you with the side of his head, body, and finally his tail.

When you come home covered with the strange smells of the outside world, your cat wants to gather information from these smells and mark you anew as a family member. You can't smell the scent from a cat's scent glands, but your cat can. The cat is also spreading *your* scent onto his fur with this rubbing behavior, so he can easily identify you as part of his cat family.

When your Himalayan scratches on his cat tree, or the new couch, he's also marking his territory. Scent glands on the underside of the paws leave the cat's personal marker on the scratched item. It also serves to remove dead nail from the cat's claws.

The Flehmen Response

Cats can smell through both their nose and mouth and have a sense best described as a cross between taste and smell. The *Jacobson's* or *vomeronasal* organ is situated between the nose and the palate and is connected to the roof of the mouth by a duct located behind the upper incisor teeth. Cats access this sense by *flehming*. When they smell something interesting they open their mouth in a slaw-jawed grimace that brings the odors into the mouth and in contact with the vomeronasal organ. The organ gathers tiny chemical molecules from the odors which it transmits directly to the brain. We don't clearly understand this organ's purpose but researchers think it's sexual in nature.

Spraying

Cat also use urine to mark territory, and this annoying but normal behavior has caused plenty of friction between humans and felines (see page 37). The cat backs up to a vertical surface, raises his tail and sprays urine onto the surface. The cat isn't being bad or spiteful when he does this. He's merely telling other cats that this is his territory and they'd better stay away. It can also be a sign the cat feels threatened.

Vocal Communication

Since Himalayans have Siamese— a notably vocal breed—in their background, Himalayans use a variety of meows, murmurs, yowls, and screams to communicate. You can interpret these as greetings, demands, pleas, complaints, or challenges, depending on the tone. Himalayans often "talk" when they want something, and it's up

Himalayans have strong hunting instincts. When stalking prey, your Himalayan crouches low in the grass. His eyes dilate and his tail twitches with excitement.

to you to figure out what. As you become acquainted with your Himalayan, you'll become familiar with his vocabulary and know when he wants to eat, play, be petted, and just be left alone to sleep in the sun.

Purring

There's nothing more pleasant than a lap full of purring Himalayan. Purring is the most recognized feline sound, and some researchers theorize it's caused by unsynchronized movements of the muscles of the diaphragm and the larynx. Not everyone agrees with this theory, and no one really knows for sure.

Himalayan kittens begin purring a few days after birth. The queen also purrs when the kittens are nursing, possibly to reassure and comfort the kittens, or just because she enjoys the process. Kittens can feel as well as hear their mother's purring, so purring may also act as a dinner bell. As adults, Himalayans purr when they are contented, pleased to see their humans or their cat friends, or when hungry.

Sealpoint Himalayan. Himalayans, like all cats, love to play. Provide yours with a variety of cat toys.

Cats also purr when they are ill, in labor, frightened, or dying. Cat behaviorists now believe cats purr in response to any strong emotion.

Growling

Growling is an aggressive warning. Although cats sometimes growl playfully as dogs do, the body language shows whether the cat is sincerely angry. The sound can range from a low grumble to an open mouthed yowling growl that shows that the cat feels threatened and is ready to take offense. Growling can progress to full-scale screams of rage or fear if the encroacher doesn't retreat.

Body Language

Cats use body postures to communicate their intentions and emotions. By watching the body language you can gauge his feelings. A cat's ears are especially significant in assessing his mood, and a cat's ear and head posture often precedes body stance when showing emotion. Twitching the ears back so the inner ear faces backward means irritation, but could also mean the cat is listening to sounds behind him. A cat's hearing is attuned to high-pitched sound frequencies because of the noises mice and birds make. The cat's ears are marvelously flexible and swivel to catch sounds even when the cat is asleep.

A friendly, confident Himalayan walks with his ears forward and his tail held high. The tip of the tail sometimes curves slightly to form a furry question mark shape.

A submissive cat, when faced with a stronger opponent, signals submission by making himself as small as possible. He cringes low to protect the vulnerable underbelly. The ears and whiskers flatten and the tail is held close to the ground. A submissive cat sometimes rolls onto his back, exposing his tender belly to show submis-

Himalayans can form close, loving relationships with one another, and will keep each other company when you're away.

sion and plead for mercy. A cat also does this when he's relaxed and feeling trusting toward you.

A frightened, defensive cat arches his back, turns his body sideways in relation to his attacker, flattens his ears and bristles his fur to give the impression of size and ferociousness.

An aggressive, angry cat crouches low to the ground, tail swishing angrily, paw raised to lash out. As aggression increases, the ears swivel and flatten until the back of the ears are displayed. Never pet or pick up a cat in either the aggressive or defensive posture. A terrified or angry cat might not recognize you and may lash out.

Hunting and Predation

Cats are carnivores and have an instinctive desire to hunt. When your cat leaps on your toes or stalks a cat toy, he is practicing hunting skills. While not all cats learn to be good hunters, they all have the instinctual desire. Hunger doesn't trigger the hunting instinct, so making cats go hungry won't turn them into better mousers. In fact, studies show well-nourished cats make better hunters than undernourished ones.

Cats habitually hunt at night when their prey is active. That's why your Himalayan races around when you're trying to sleep. It's a myth that cats can see in the dark, but cats do use the available light much more efficiently than do humans. They need only one-sixth of our illumination level to see clearly. When your Himalayan's eyes shine, you're seeing light bouncing off a layer of cells behind the retina called the *tapetum lucidum*. This special light-conserving mechanism allows the cat to see in neardarkness.

How Cats Hunt

When hunting, a cat conceals himself in a place that gives him a good view of the hunting area. For example, a cat might crouch in a stand of tall grass or at the base of a wall. When he sights his prey, he crouches low. His eyes dilate. He then creeps forward very slowly and silently, pausing often to watch his intended prey. Only the tip of the tail twitches to show the cat's excitement. He prepares to pounce by tensing, shifting weight to his toes, and treading with his back feet. Finally, he springs, pinning the prey with his front feet, and delivers the death bite to the nape.

Sometimes a cat won't kill his prey immediately but "plays" with it, releasing and recapturing the prey again and again. While this strikes us as being unduly cruel, researchers believe this behavior, like play, serves to hone the hunting skills. Since your Himalayan will be an indoor cat, you shouldn't have a problem with this behavior. Your cat will practice his hunting skills on his favorite cat toy.

Bringing Home Prey

A cat who is allowed outside may bring home prey and proudly present it to you or leave it as a "gift" on your favorite pillow. This means she accepts you as a family member. She brings you the prey so you can learn how to hunt. Carrying prey home for the kittens' education is normal behavior. The cat thinks she's teaching you by giving you an example by which to learn. Cats probably think we're terribly slow learners.

My tip: Keeping your cat inside will solve this problem. If your cat gets out and brings home prey, or catches prey inside your home, rather than recoil with distaste or punish your cat, accept the gift and profusely praise her cunning and skill. Then quietly dispose of the token as soon as possible, because rodents and birds can harbor infectious diseases and parasites.

Covering Their Tracks

You can observe another hunting-related behavior at dinnertime. When she's finished eating, your Himalayan scratches around her bowl as if trying to bury the leftovers. The first time I noticed this, I associated it with the covering of stool in the litter box. I thought my cats were saying, "I'm letting you know what this icky food smells like."

Actually, this has nothing to do with elimination, but the same reason lies behind both actions. Cats bury their wastes and their leftovers to cover their scent and to keep bigger predators or dominant members of their species from tracking them.

Acclimation and Daily Life

Preparing for Arrival

After you've made your choice and before your Himalayan arrives, make a few simple preparations. First and most important, cat-proof the house (see HOW-TO: Cat-Proofing Your Home, page 42). Second, get the equipment necessary to make your cat feel at home, and to provide for his comfort and safety.

Cat Carrier: The cheapest cat carriers are cardboard and will do in a pinch, but they aren't sturdy enough for long-term use. Stout plastic carriers are a better bet. Buy one with enough ventilation. Many plastic carriers have reinforced wire doors that allow the cat to see out and the air to get in. Wicker or wooden carriers are also available, but the plastic ones are my choice, as plastic is easier to clean if the cat has an accident, and wicker or wood are often chewed by frisky Himalayans. For frequent feline flyers, buy a carrier that fits under the plane's seat.

My tip: Ask the breeder for a familiar toy, pillow, towel, or blanket for the ride home. Put the item into the carrier with the cat. The familiar smell will be comforting, and if put in the cat's new bed, will help the cat adjust.

Cat bed: Many kinds of cat beds are available. Some cat owners feel buying a fancy cat bed is unnecessary as a cat will sleep where he wants anyway. A cardboard box piled with clean, old sheets will be as satisfactory as the fanciest velvet-lined, canopy-draped bed.

More important is *where* he sleeps. Cats are a territorial species. With that in mind, buy a cat bed that suits your taste and pocketbook, and you and your four-legged friend can discuss the placement later on. Your cat will probably abandon it and snuggle in with you, anyway.

Himalayans like the round "snuggle" type cat beds, available in pet supply stores. A small, inexpensive beanbag chair covered with a soft blanket or towel is another good option. Cats love the way it conforms to their contours. Make sure the bed and its cover are washable.

Litter box: The proper litter box is important, particularly since Himalayans should be kept indoors. While the Himalayan is a kitten, you'll

Necessary accessories: scratching equipment, food dishes, leash and collar, toys, cat bed, and cat carrier.

need a litter box shallow enough so the kitten can easily step in—three inches (8 cm) or so. As the cat grows, buy a deeper pan (up to six inches [15 cm]), to prevent the cat from scratching litter out of the pan. Regardless of the type of cat litter, remove wastes from the litter box each day, and clean the box thoroughly once a week.

Several types of cat boxes are available. They range from simple (a plastic pan) to elaborate (covered, mink-lined cottages). A litter box without a cover works best. The confining nature of a covered box makes it easier for wastes and urine to stain a Himalayan's long fur.

Litter: The appropriate kind of litter depends upon a number of factors, as discussed briefly below. You might also ask your breeder or veterinarian for advice.

Regular clay litters control odors well. The cat doesn't track them around the house as much because of their heavier weight. However, the litter's weight is also its main disadvantage (remember—lift with your knees). Since the litter must be replaced continuously, the cost can add up, particularly in a multi-cat home.

Clumping clay litters containing sodium bentonite (a clay that swells and clumps together when it encounters fluid) are popular because these litters "cement" the cat's urine into easily removable clumps. They help control odors and are economical. However, some cat owners who use clumping clay litters have reported health problems in their cats, including respiratory and intestinal conditions. These problems seem particularly severe in young cats and kittens. For this reason, I recommend clumping litters only for adult cats. Use a low-dust clumping litter, because cats and humans alike can inhale the dust. If you have asthma or other respiratory problems, consult your doctor before using clumping litters, or any litter that produces fine dust. One of the newer biodegradable plant-based litters may be a better choice if you or your cat have health concerns. Plant-based litters are available at the larger pet supply stores and some health food stores. These earth-friendly litters are made of various combinations of wheat, corn, recycled paper, alfalfa, cedar, or citrus.

Dishes: Cat dishes are available at pet supply stores in plastic, metal, ceramic, or glass. There's no reason why you can't use dishes designed for humans, though. These are often cheaper and are usually free of lead-

Sealpoint Himalayan. According to CFA's breed registration totals, the Himalayan is the most popular breed in the United States today.

Flamepoint (red) Himalayan.

based glazes, which is important as lead can leech into the food and water and poison a cat. I use heavy, shallow ceramic bowls. They are heavy enough to keep my cats from pushing them all over the kitchen floor or toppling them in their feeding frenzy. Avoid plastic dishes because they can contribute to feline acne. Choose a dish that is wide and flat enough to accommodate the Himalayan's wide face and long whiskers.

Place the dishes in a convenient, easily accessible area. The kitchen is a good choice. To make cleanup easier, put a plastic place mat under the dishes. Don't locate the litter box near the dishes as cats don't like to eliminate where they eat and may avoid the litter box.

Ask the breeder what cat food he or she recommends. If you wish to change foods when you bring the kitten home, gradually switch from the old food to prevent stomach upset or diarrhea.

Grooming supplies: These are vital to keep a Himalayan's coat in good shape. See the grooming supply list (page 45).

Scratching equipment: Provide an outlet for the Himalayan's natural desire to scratch. If no scratching post is available, your cat companion will satisfy his urge by shredding the couch, chairs, or stereo speakers.

Scratching equipment comes in a variety of styles, shapes, and price ranges, from simple scratching pads that lie on the floor or hang from a doorknob, to elaborate carpet-covered skyscrapers. Let your pocketbook be your guide. The post must have a sturdy base, so it will not tip over and frighten the cat into scratching elsewhere.

Carpeting is not a feline's favorite scratching material, so buy a cat post that provides other scratching mediums as well. Sisal fiber rope is an excellent choice, as is natural bark. Again, your pocketbook and taste should guide you. A piece of carpeting, turned with the jute backing facing up, makes a cheap alternative. Place the post near a sunny window or draft-free corner. If you put the post in an out-of-the-way place, the cat may shun it for the couch closer to his favorite human. Rub the post with catnip to spark the cat's interest.

Cat toys: These, too, come in great variety, and you'll probably find the cat will get as much pleasure from wadded paper balls as from the most expensive cat toy—if you are there to share the fun.

Cat toys provoke a Himalayan's hunting instincts, which they practice through play. Rubber balls that roll tantalizingly along the floor, feathers on string that whir in the air, and knit-

ted catnip toys to carry around will all be a hit. Avoid toys with attached string (including elastic), unless all play is supervised and the toys put away promptly when finished.

My tip: You can make inexpensive cat toys easily. Stuff large, old tube socks with catnip and batting or, if you're into recycling, clothes dryer lint. (**Note:** don't use dryer lint from wash loads in which you used fabric softeners or bleach.) These toys don't even require sewing. Just tie a knot in the sock's end and you're set. When the toy becomes soiled and the catnip no longer potent, simply unstuff the sock, toss it in the washer and dryer, and fill again with fresh materials. My cats love this kind of toy. They proudly drag them around the house like freshly captured prey.

Collars: Your cat will only need a collar if he is allowed outdoors (a very bad idea), or if you plan to teach him to walk on a lead. If allowed outdoors, he will need a collar with identification, as well as a flea collar. Buy the "break-away" elastic type; if the collar gets caught, the elastic breaks to keep the cat from strangling.

My tip: If you keep your Himalayan indoors at all times, you won't need a collar. If you plan to show your cat, be aware that a collar can chafe and leave marks that can cost you points in the show ring.

Finding a Veterinarian

Before picking up the cat, choose a veterinarian. Your veterinarian should have ample experience in caring for small domestic animals (as opposed to livestock or exotics), be close by, and provide some kind of 24-hour emergency service or referral. Ask around. Your fellow cat owners, your breeder, or humane society personnel may have recommendations.

Veterinarians who specialize in feline medicine usually have the equip-

Involving your children in the care of your Himalayan will help them understand that cats are living beings. Be sure your children know how to hold your Himalayan.

ment and expertise to give excellent care to Himalayans. At any rate, your veterinarian should be up-to-date, compassionate, and willing to answer all your questions. The office should be clean, well maintained, and free of unpleasant odors. The support staff should be knowledgeable and caring. It's important to make an appointment to meet the veterinarian personally before his or her services are needed.

Bringing Home Baby

When ready to pick up your new Himalayan, schedule a veterinary appointment for examination and testing. Some breeders furnish a certificate for the cat's first examination. This exam is particularly important if you are adding to an existing cat family because you don't want to bring home a contagious disease. To be on the safe side, have the examination before allowing the cat to mingle with his new companions.

Pick up the kitten when you can spend time together, such as just before the weekend. The breeder will probably provide a veterinarian's certificate stating that the kitten is in good health, a record of his birthdate and vaccinations, registration papers for his or her cat association, and (unless withheld until altering) a copy of the kitten's pedigree. The breeder may also give you written instructions to help with the kitten's adjustment, a "kitten kit" containing cat food coupons, information on grooming, feeding instructions, and so forth.

When you arrive home, set the carrier in a quiet place and allow the cat to get used to the new sights and smells. At first, the new arrival will feel vulnerable and uncertain. When the cat calms, he will be curious about his new home. When you think he's ready, let him out of the carrier into the room. Allow him to explore, giving him as much time as he needs to feel comfortable. Stay quiet and don't make sudden movements. It's very tempting to handle the kitten at this point, but restrain yourself. The kitten needs to feel in control of this new, frightening situation. Give the kitten the opportunity to check out his new litter box. If you have other cats or pets, keep them away for now.

When the kitten has completely explored the room, allow him to settle down and gain confidence before you allow him into the rest of the house. When the cat begins to groom, that means he feels comfortable. Offer your new Himalayan food and water, allow him to sleep if he wishes, and give him plenty of love and attention (but that doesn't mean harass him). Introduce him to his new bed, scratching post, toys, and dishes.

Handling Your Himalayan

Some Himalayans will allow you to hold them on their backs, and some even like it. Your Himalayan will let you know what he prefers. If he wiggles, cries, or looks unhappy, try a different position. Never pick up a cat by the scruff of the neck; in an adult cat that can cause serious harm. It's okay to hold a cat down by grasping the scruff, particularly when restraining an angry or frightened cat.

To pick up a Himalayan, put one hand under the front legs and scoop the cat up with the other hand under the rear quarters.

Support the rear legs and bring the cat up into the crook of your arm, with one hand holding the cat's chest.

Kittens and Kids

Children as well as adults feel the need for an animal friend, one that loves them unconditionally and is always there for them, a nonjudgmental companion in which they can confide. A cat companion can also be a great way for a child to learn responsibility and parenting skills.

Enlist your children's cooperation in helping the kitten adapt by having them sit beside the carrier and visit the kitten quietly. When you let the kitten out, have your children keep an eye on him as he explores his new environment. Keep away children who are too young to understand how to treat a kitten. The kitten needs quiet time to adapt to this new environment.

Children need to be taught that pets are not toys, but rather living creatures with feelings and rights of their own. Teach your children how to treat

Himalayans make perfect housecats. They are well-suited to life in an apartment or home.

cats and other animals. Include your children in your cat's daily care and grooming, and they will form a close bond of friendship that will last throughout your cat's life.

Teach your children how to hold the cat. A kitten's rib cage is very soft, and rough treatment can cause fractures and internal injuries. Rough handling can also cause the cat to bite or scratch in self-defense.

The Adjustment Period

When the cat has thoroughly explored his new environment and feels comfortable (usually several hours to several days after introduction), it's time to get acquainted. The kitten will want to get to know you. Set aside some time to win over your new Himalayan friend.

Cats love and obey humans they trust. To build the closest relationship possible, show the cat he can rely on you to behave acceptably. This means not holding him when he doesn't wish to be held (except, of course, during bath time), never abusing him, and always providing him with love, diversion, and attention. Cats can sense your feelings, and will meet you halfway when given a chance.

Teaching Your Himalayan

As a general rule, it's easy to teach a Himalayan how you want him to behave. Cats are user friendly; their habits coincide very well with ours. They are clean, and quiet. The Himalayan, in particular, is an adaptable and easygoing companion.

Contrary to popular belief, cats are not too independent or dumb to learn. Just exercise patience, consistency, persistence, and positive reinforcement. Praise will get you much farther than punishment. The only thing a cat learns from punishment is to avoid you, and there goes the chance at a close, trusting relationship.

Tortiepoint Himalayan. Torties have a patchwork of seal, red and/or cream on the point areas.

No cat is born knowing how to behave, and your cat will make mistakes at first. Cats, like humans, go through a period of adolescence when they are active and mischievous. They seem to think they're immortal when they stick their noses into boiling pots and nibble on electrical cords. Exercise patience and care so you and your cat can survive this period.

Scratching Problems

Cats have a natural need to scratch, and it's frustrating to watch the cat use the new couch as a scratching post. Rather than punish him, however, give him substitutes to scratch upon and teach him to use them (see page 29). When your cat begins scratching at a forbidden spot, say "No!" and put him on his post or pad. When he uses the post correctly, praise him. Give him a treat. He will get the idea.

Cats also scratch out of boredom. Providing the cat with toys and diversions will help. Keeping a cat's nails clipped helps, too (see Grooming, page 45).

If your Himalayan continues scratching in inappropriate places, try rubbing the post with catnip to make it more appealing. Make the problem areas less attractive by putting double-sided tape or aluminum foil on the floor below the scratching area (for example, at the base of the couch or chair).

Tape inflated balloons to the problem areas. When a cat pops one with his claws, he will avoid scratching there again. However, only try this when you're home, so you can pick up the balloon pieces before the cat eats them.

My tip: Sometimes, you can resolve scratching post avoidance by moving the post to a new location. Your Himalayan may not like the location (if, for example, another cat has "claimed" the area). By moving the post, you provide the cat with options.

Declawing

Declawing domestic cats to prevent scratching problems is controversial. Some countries, such as Britain and Germany, have outlawed the practice as barbaric and unnecessary. Many United States breeders, veterinarians, cat registries, and cat associations feel the same way. If you plan on showing your Himalayan, be aware that most cat organizations forbid declawed cats in both the purebred and household pet categories.

Declawing removes the germinal cells and some or all of the terminal

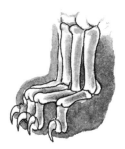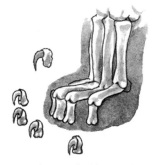

Declawing removes the terminal bone of the claw and the claw tip.

bone in the toe, similar to cutting off a human's fingers at the first joint. Usually, only the front claws are removed, since the front claws are the ones that cause the most damage to furniture and possessions. The surgery requires general anesthesia and the cat is subject to the risks anesthesia entails.

Declawing removes a cat's ability to defend himself and to climb to avoid attackers; therefore, declawed cats must be kept inside. Also, some cat owners say they noticed personality changes in their cats, including failure to use the litter box appropriately, after the surgery.

Some people, however, feel declawing is acceptable in certain circumstances. As one veterinarian puts it, declawing a cat is probably less harmful than constantly badgering the cat whenever he tries satisfying his normal urge to scratch.

The American Veterinary Medical Association's current position is "declawing of domestic cats is justifiable *when the cat cannot be trained to refrain from using its claws destructively.*"

Since cats can be taught to use a scratching post, make every effort to do so before resorting to surgical alteration. Keeping the cat's claws trimmed will also help minimize the damage the cat can inflict (see Nail Trimming, page 47).

A product called Soft Paws Nail Caps for cats provides another option. These soft vinyl caps are applied over the cat's trimmed nails and held in place with adhesive, effectively blunting the claws and making damage to belongings impossible. The caps last until the nail grows out, about four to eight weeks. Your veterinarian applies the first set and provides training. The initial application and training costs around $30 and includes a supply of the nail caps. From then on, you can do the application. Usage can be stopped whenever you wish.

Nail caps are positive, painless, and safe alternatives to declawing. The nail tips are harmless even if swallowed, and come in several decorator colors. See your veterinarian for more information.

Dealing with Cat Hair

It's a fact of life—you must accept cat hair as one of the prices of cat ownership. You'll find it on the bed, the couch, and all over the carpet, or as little eddies under foot on the kitchen floor. Himalayans do not shed more than shorthaired cats; they just have longer, more noticeable hair. Still, what to do about the cat hair covering everything you own is a hairy problem.

You can take steps that, while not eliminating the problem, will at least reduce it to a manageable level. This is particularly important if you or a family member is allergic to cats.

Cat hair is not what produces allergic symptoms in humans. Rather, it's an allergenic protein called Fel d1 secreted via saliva and sebaceous glands. When cats groom their fur, they spread Fel d1 onto their hair. Regular bathing reduces the Fel d1 covering the cat's fur, thereby reducing allergic symptoms.

Simply, the steps to curb the cat hair curse are: cover, vacuum, dust, comb, bathe, and train. Cover the most frequently used surfaces upon which your cat will sit or sleep. For example, if the Himalayan's cat bed isn't washable (a bad idea in the first place), or is a bother to wash, put a piece of flannel sheet, a bit of washable blanket, or other such material in the bed to make cleaning up easy. The back of the couch seems to be a popular perching post for Himalayans, so cut down vacuuming time by covering the back of the couch with a washable "throw" or blanket.

My tip: I cover my bed comforter with a washable comforter (duvet)

A squirt bottle is a painless, effective training tool. However never squirt your Himalayan with anything other than water. Don't use a squirt bottle that previously contained toxic fluids.

cover so I can simply throw the cover into the wash.

Combing a Himalayan regularly will go far in curbing the curse of the cat hair (see Grooming, page 45). Removing the loose hairs on the cat will reduce the hair covering your belongings. In addition, regular vacuuming and dusting, as disagreeable as these chores are, will help reduce the amount of cat hair around.

Train your Himalayan to stay off the counters, kitchen table, couches, beds, and other areas you want kept clean of cat hair. Use the squirt bottle method: fill a plastic squirt bottle with cool water, and give him a brief squirt when he is someplace forbidden. Cats learn quickly to avoid the unpleasant water, and do not as readily associate the correction with you. By the way, the squirt bottle method may be used in other training as well. Also available are training devices that keep a pet off forbidden areas with annoying sounds or static shocks. These work even when you're not around. Buy one that is guaranteed safe for cats.

Sealpoint Himalayan. No matter what the coat color, the Himalayan's eyes are always blue. However, the shade and intensity varies.

Litter Box Problems

Litter box avoidance is one of the most frequent and irritating "disagreements" humans have with felines. Inappropriate urination or defecation means a cat is trying to tell you something. Cats use elimination as communication (a kind of E-mail, if you will). A new pet or person, a move or change in schedule, overcrowding, a conflict with another cat, or even a dirty litter box can cause the cat to eliminate inappropriately.

If the cat urinates or defecates outside the litter box, schedule an appointment with the veterinarian. Urinary tract infections can cause inappropriate urination (see Health Care, page 68). If the veterinarian rules out a physical problem, take a look at what's going on in the cat's life. Recognizing the reasons for litter box avoidance will help you find a solution.

A common reason for litter box avoidance is the cat's natural cleanliness. A dirty litter box can make the cat turn up his nose and look for a private corner in which to do his business. There's a good reason for this. Predators and dominant cats locate by scent and a dirty litter box makes cats nervous. (Dominant cats leave their wastes uncovered to mark their territory.) Try changing the litter more often—once a week is usually sufficient, but some cats aren't comfortable with that. Scoop the solid wastes and soiled litter daily.

If a change in behavior occurs after switching brands of litter, try changing back. Your cat may not like the new litter. Some litters are highly perfumed and are offensive to some cats. Other litters just don't have the right "feel." Experiment with various litters, or try mixing several kinds. Don't mix clumping and non-clumping litters.

Seal Lynxpoint Himalayan. Lynxpoint Himalayans have tabby markings on their point areas.

Location, location, location, just as in real estate, is important to successful litter box training. If your cat doesn't like the litter box's placement, he may avoid it. Put the litter box in an area that allows the cat privacy, but is convenient for cleaning. Some people prefer keeping the box in the bathroom, but in a multi-cat household that could get crowded. I use a closet in the spare bedroom, lined with plastic to make cleanup easier.

Some cats don't like sharing their litter box with other cats. Provide one box for each. The size, shape, and depth can also affect the cat's behavior. Try another size or type.

Male and female cats spray to mark their territory (see page 23). Spaying and neutering will most likely eliminate this problem if you do it before the spraying becomes a habit. If a cat continues spraying after neutering, it can mean something is wrong. For example, even spayed or neutered cats may spray if another cat is threatening their territory. My most persistent sprayer is a spayed female.

Male cats, and sometimes females too, mark their territory by spraying urine onto vertical surfaces. Altering usually eliminates this behavior.

Punishing a cat will not solve the problem. That will only teach the cat to eliminate when you're not around. Since cats locate their litter box by scent, rubbing the cat's nose in the urine will only teach the cat that this is a good spot to urinate. Addressing the problem's cause will end the unacceptable behavior. Ask your veterinarian or breeder for advice if you're stumped for a solution.

Spaying and Neutering

Preventing unwanted pregnancy is the most important reason to spay or neuter cats, but altering has behavioral advantages as well.

1. Early altering means a cat won't display the restlessness, yowling, spraying, and other sexual behaviors inherent to unaltered cats.

2. Altering benefits a cat's health as well; intact females have a seven times greater risk of mammary cancer than neutered females.

3. Spaying also eliminates all uterine infections.

4. Neutering reduces aggressive behavior in males. If your neutered cat gets outside, he will get in fewer cat fights and will stay closer to home.

5. Neutering's biggest benefit is the reduction of the hormone levels that prompt spraying.

Neuter your Himalayan as early as possible before the sexual behaviors become lifelong habits. The risks are small compared to the benefits and you'll be doing the cat population a favor by preventing surplus kittens. Spaying and neutering is inexpensive compared to feeding, raising, providing veterinary care, and finding good homes for progressive litters of kittens.

Contrary to popular belief, altering will not make your cat fat and lazy. Only too much food and too little exercise will do that. Nor will having one litter calm a female Himalayan. Himalayans usually need no such calming, anyway.

The American Humane Association reports that between 5.9 and 9.9 million cats are euthanized in shelters each year. It is vital that all cat owners (and dog owners, too) spay and neuter their pets. Two cats and their subsequent offspring, left unaltered, can produce more than 150,000 kittens within seven years! We don't have enough good homes for them all. Please, be a responsible pet owner and alter your pets.

Spending Time with Your Himalayan

Himalayans are playful, social animals that need love and attention if they are to live long, happy lives. Plan on spending a few quality minutes a day combing, cuddling, and capering with your Himmie. This shouldn't be difficult because your cat companion makes entertaining, enjoyable company. It doesn't really matter when; your cat will adjust to your timetable. Most likely, he is well aware of your schedule. He knows when you are available and receptive to playing or snuggling. Of course, your idea of "available and receptive" may not be the same as your cat's. To your feline friend, 3:00 A.M. seems a splendid time to play. After all, you're not doing anything else at the moment.

Of course, you need to keep a fixed feeding schedule for your cat. A regular schedule will assure that you don't feed the cat too much or too often (see Nutrition, page 55). Once the feeding schedule is in place, your Himalayan will remind you loudly if you forget.

My tip: Think of ways to involve the cat in daily activities. For example, my cats get several informal grooming sessions each week while I'm getting ready for work. I keep their grooming supplies under the sink in the bathroom, and because they enjoy their combing, they follow me in. That way we all get our hair done at the same time. I also spend time with my cats while I'm working. I keep a folded blanket on the floor beside my chair so my kitties can visit with me in comfort while I work (okay, so my cats are a little spoiled).

Adding a Second Cat

If you are going to get two Himalayan kittens, get them both at the same time. They'll play together when you're not around, and continue to enjoy each other's company even when they're adults.

If you want to add a second kitten after your Himalayan has grown, follow the new kitten adjustment guidelines (see page 31). After the adjustment period, the cats will usually settle their differences and learn to at least tolerate each other. Buying a kitten of a different breed shouldn't be a problem unless the breed is a very active one (see page 13).

Introducing adult cats to one another is more challenging, but certainly possible.

Cats need company and love. Two Himalayans will provide entertainment and companionship for each other when you're away.

• Don't toss two adult cats into a room and expect them to sort things out—most likely this will make them hate each other forever.
• Don't leave them alone together until you're sure they've declared a cease-fire.
• Allow them time to get used to each other. As with people, the first impression is lasting.
• If possible, put new cats in a room with glass doors that can be closed so your other cats can see and smell the new arrival in safety.
• If they do fight, don't try to separate them with your bare hands. In the heat of battle they may not recognize you as a friend and could hurt you. Throw a rug or big towel between them, clap your hands, or squirt them with a water bottle. Put them in separate rooms as soon as you can do so safely. Check them both carefully for wounds (see Abscesses, page 75).

The process may take time, but be patient. Shower both cats with affection and attention. They will usually come to an understanding. If not, you may have to find a home for the new arrival.

Environmental Hazards

Outdoor Hazards

It's a jungle out there—the outside world is full of hazards. Cars, of course, are a major threat, and are the main reason an outdoor cat has a much shorter life expectancy than one kept indoors. An indoor cat can live 10, 15, or even 20 years. An outdoor cat, on average, won't celebrate her tenth birthday.

Cars pose other hazards beside auto accidents. Outside cats, searching for warm sleeping places on cold days, will sometimes crawl up inside car engine compartments. The cat can be badly injured or killed when the car's owner unknowingly starts the car.

Automotive fluids are harmful to cats. In particular, antifreeze containing ethylene glycol is extremely dangerous for cats and other animals—less than a teaspoon will kill. The antifreeze itself is not the cause of death. The antifreeze is converted into a toxic substance called oxalic acid when the liver attempts to metabolize the antifreeze. It's the oxalic acid that causes the damage.

For some reason, antifreeze attracts animals. Often cited is antifreeze's sweet taste, but since cats cannot taste sweets, another reason must exist for the attraction. Since it is colorless and odorless, perhaps cats mistake it for water. Whatever the reason, keep antifreeze away from your cat, including the pools that accumulate under your car from a leaking radiator (see Poisoning, page 82).

My tip: New antifreezes now on the market contain propylene glycol, a chemical that works like ethylene glycol but is much less toxic to animals.

Even if your cat is an indoor-only cat, the neighborhood cats and other animals would benefit from your using these products. Ask for these products at auto supply stores. Check the ingredient list carefully.

Prey Animals

Cats are predators, and an outside cat will occasionally catch and kill rodents, birds, and other small animals. This is generally not cause for concern (except for the prey). However, your cat can acquire parasites, such as worms and fleas, as well as diseases from prey animals. Take prey away from your cat as soon as possible. Better yet, keep your cat inside.

Other Animals

Other cats, dogs, and wildlife can be hazardous to your cat's health. Not every cat makes it up a tree when chased by a dog. Dog attacks account for a sizable number of cat injuries and deaths each year. Also, other cats can injure your Himalayan severely (and vice versa) if they battle over territory, which even altered cats occasionally do. Since deep fang and claw puncture wounds can easily become infected, check your cat's body carefully for puncture wounds if your cat escapes and gets in a fight. These puncture wounds are often small and hard to see (see Abscesses, page 75).

Casual contact between felines can spread many diseases and parasites. Keep your cat's vaccinations current, and check your cat often for parasites. Your Himalayan's long coat is an attractive home for pesky parasites.

Arnold Schwartzakatz, a bluepoint Himalayan male, survived his encounter with the bumper of a car. Your Himalayan may not be so fortunate. For his protection, your Himalayan should be allowed outdoors only when supervised.

Wildlife is dangerous, not only because animals can be reservoirs for disease and parasites, but because cats can become prey as well. Coyotes, bobcats, cougars, eagles, bears, and other animals will prey on domestic cats if one happens across their path. Cats can tangle with wildlife risking injury and, in the case of skunks, a foul-smelling surprise. Also, rabies is a common disease among skunks.

Human Hazards

People can be dangerous, too. Pet theft is a thriving business in the United States today. Purebred animals are particularly targeted because purebreds can be resold for a profit. However, thieves steal random-bred cats and dogs as well. People called "batchers" make their living stealing pets from residential streets and selling them to medical research facilities, representing the animals as strays. Cats are also stolen for bait in the

training of guard dogs and hunting hawks.

Despite efforts to outlaw steel jaw leg-hold traps, these devices are still used in certain areas, and cats fall victim. When caught in this trap, the animal dies a slow and agonizing death. Cats wandering into hunting areas can be mistaken for rabbits or other small game.

Cats who become nuisances can be subject to retribution by neighbors. Some people just don't like cats, and are entitled to their opinions. Your relationship with such neighbors will be more positive, and you will promote the cat crusade everywhere, if you show you're a responsible cat owner.

Some cat owners feel we shouldn't deny cats the opportunity to exercise their instincts, and enjoy the fresh air, sunshine, and diversion the great outdoors provides. They feel the trade-off is worth the risk—a short, stimulating life is better than a long, boring one.

HOW-TO:
Cat-Proofing Your Home

Before your Himalayan comes home, take a few minutes to check for hazards. Seemingly innocent items can spell trouble when you add a Himalayan to the mix. Cats are for the most part smart and savvy survivors (they haven't survived for this many years by leaping off cliffs, lemming style), but a few precautions will make your Himalayan safer and ease your mind.

Kitchen/pantry: As a general rule, keep dishwashers, freezers, refrigerators, ovens, and microwaves closed when not in use. Himalayans are particularly interested in appliances used to store food. Unplug appliances like blenders, toasters, electric kettles, irons, hot plates, etc, when you're finished with them. One of my cats once turned on my blender by stepping on the buttons; fortunately I was home at the time! Cats also some-

times chew on electrical wiring (particularly when they are young) and can be electrocuted. The exposed wiring can also cause fires.

Supervise stove tops when they are in use. Cover garbage cans, particularly cans used to dispose of bones or other food wastes, because these can be dangerous, and in some cases deadly for your cat. For example, the preservative benzoic acid used in human foods is extremely toxic to cats.

Secure cupboards and drawers holding hazardous materials such as bleach, disinfectants, solvents, cleaners (particularly those containing phenol), insect sprays, and ant, mouse, or rat poisons.

Bathrooms: Secure the medicine cabinet. Cats are sensitive to some common medications that are safe for humans, such as aspirin and acetaminophen. One acetaminophen tablet can kill a cat. Since pills, being small and round, make tempting toys for your Himalayan,

Keep dryers closed when not in use.

keep pills and vitamins in their bottles with the caps tightly closed until you are ready to take them. Unplug and put away hair dryers, electric razors, and so forth when not in use. Keep the toilet lid down if you use dissolving chemicals in the tank to keep the toilet bowl clean.

Laundry room: Dryers can be dangerous for cats. Warm, clean clothes attract cats and your Himalayan may crawl in for a nap. It's a good idea to count cat noses before you start dryers. Don't leave hot irons unattended. Cats investigate objects by smelling them and cats have burned their delicate noses by sniffing irons and other hot objects.

Living areas: Put breakables and valuables you can't live without out of reach or in display cases. Cover electrical cords and disconnect them when not in use. If your cat has a spraying problem, cover unused electrical outlets with plastic inserts (available at hardware stores). Screen fireplaces and heaters. Use candles, kerosene lamps, and other fire sources only when you can supervise them.

Craft/hobby room: Unplug hot glue guns, soldering irons, and sewing machines. Put

What's wrong with this picture? Himalayans, like all cats, are curious. It's important to protect them from household hazards.

away sewing and craft supplies when not in use. String enteritis results from swallowing string-like items. Needles with attached thread can be dangerous. The thread gets caught around the base of the tongue while the rest passes into the stomach and intestine. This causes vomiting, diarrhea, dehydration, and depression as the intestines contract in an attempt to pass the string. This leads to death if the string lacerates the curving intestinal tract walls. Store any potentially toxic material (paints, glues, varnish) in a secure area.

Gardening supplies: Store fertilizers, insecticides, pesticides, herbicides, pool chemicals, and bait poisons (particularly those containing warfarin and strychnine) in areas to which your cat has no access. Cats can be poisoned in four ways: by ingesting the chemical directly; by rubbing against the containers that are stained with

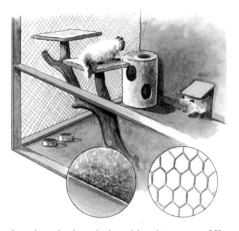

A secure cat-run equipped with a cat door allowing passage to the inside provides your Himalayan with safe access to the great outdoors.

the chemical and absorbing it through the skin or licking it off the fur; by breathing the fumes; and by walking through the chemical (such as with lawn chemicals) and then licking the chemical off the paws.

Darkrooms: Film processing solutions, particularly those containing ethylene glycol (the same chemical that's in antifreeze), are deadly to cats. Keep cats out.

Miscellaneous: Screen all windows that will be kept open if you live above the first floor. Balconies should be off limits; some cats do not have good sense about heights and may fall.

Some houseplants are poisonous to cats. See the list below to be sure you don't have poisonous varieties. The list only mentions the more common poisonous varieties, and, of course, many of these and other poisonous plants can be found outside as well as in your home. Usually, cats have good sense when it comes to avoiding poisonous plants, but indoor cats may eat poisonous varieties because of the limited availability of edible greens. Because cats like to nibble greenery, it's a good idea to provide your cat with a safe substitute, such as oat grass.

To protect your house plants put them on high shelves or hang them from the ceiling. Cover the potting soil in indoor planters so that your cat does not use them as litter boxes.

Plants Poisonous to Cats

Amaryllis	Hemlock	Moonseed
Azalea	Henbane	Morning glory
Bird of paradise	Holly	Mushrooms
Belladonna	Honeysuckle	Nightshade
Black locust	Hydrangea	Nutmeg
Caladium	Indian tobacco	Oleander
Castor bean	Iris	Periwinkle
Chinaberry	Ivy	Peyote
Daffodil	Jack-in-the-pulpit	Philodendron
Daphne	Jerusalem cherry	Potato
Datura	Jimson weed	Rhododendron
Dieffenbachia	Larkspur	Rhubarb
Elephant's ear	Lily of the valley	Skunk cabbage
Euonymus	Marijuana	Tobacco
Foxglove	Mescal bean	Tulip
Fruit pits	Mistletoe	Wisteria
Golden chain	Monkshood	Yew

Sealpoint Himalayan. Indoor cats are not always protected from fleas. Regular grooming will alert you to flea infestation.

I very much disagree with this attitude. Cats are domestic animals who depend upon us for protection. They are not wild animals and do not have the necessary skills to survive outdoors, particularly in these hazardous times. When you take into consideration the dangers to which your cat is exposed, and the damage that feral cats can cause to existing ecosystems, there's no justification to allowing domestic cats to roam free.

Cats adapt extremely well to the indoors if you provide them with exercise and mental stimulation. Keeping cats indoors is the responsible thing to do. Even people who love cats don't necessarily like them using their gardens for litter boxes. I want my cats to lead long, healthy lives, so I keep them inside. Weigh the pros and cons, evaluate your lifestyle and area, and decide what's best for you and your cat.

Indoor Hazards

Keeping your Himalayan inside doesn't mean she is completely safe. Himalayans, with their agile paws and inquiring minds, find ways to get into mischief. Cats have a poor ability to detoxify their systems and excrete poisonous substances. They rely upon their prey's bodies to do that for them. Even small amounts of toxic substances can kill your cat. Cats are like children—if you want them to stay away from something, they will make a beeline for it as soon as you turn your back, or even while you're looking. Of course, no one can plan for every contingency but if you take a few simple precautions outlined in the HOW-TO section (page 42), you can make sure curiosity *doesn't* kill the cat.

Grooming Your Himalayan

Cats are naturally clean animals and devote a good portion of their day to grooming. A cat's tongue, covered with hooked, backward-pointing scales, is useful for combing the fur and skin. Longhaired breeds like the Himalayan, however, require considerable help to keep looking sharp.

A regular grooming program is good for your cat's health. Combing removes dead hair that can form hair balls in the cat's stomach (as well as cover your couch), gets rid of dead skin and dander, stimulates the skin, tones muscle, and encourages blood circulation. If groomed regularly, your cat will have fewer hairballs (see page 68). Grooming is also a good time to examine your Himalayan for health problems so you can attend to them in their early stages.

Grooming involves more than combing the cat's fur. The cat's nails, ears, eyes, and teeth need attention, too. Grooming can be a pleasant experience for you and your cat, if you train him to tolerate handling when he's young. Establish a daily grooming program before the cat is three months old. Your Himalayan will come to expect and even enjoy his grooming sessions if you make the experience pleasant with praise, cuddles, and hugs.

Grooming Products

Combs: The most important grooming tool is a good-quality stainless steel comb with teeth about 1¼ inches (3.2 cm) long. One end has teeth very close together; the other end has teeth farther apart. The Greyhound Comb, available at pet and grooming supply stores, is favored by professional groomers. These combs effectively remove dead and loose hairs, and don't damage the Himalayan's beautiful fur. Combs coated with teflon are also available. These prevent static electricity from building up during the grooming session. A grooming rake is also a good investment. This comb looks much like a miniature rake (thus the name), and is easier to handle.

Other items: Other necessary items are "mat breakers" (some breeders use a sewing seam ripper for this job), tearless cat shampoo, and blunt tip scissors

Bluepoint Himalayan. Your Himalayan will learn to accept being groomed if you exercise patience and persistence.

for cutting stubborn mats. Also needed are cat nail clippers, a child-size tooth brush, and hairball preventative. Optional supplies include grooming powder (you can also use baby powder), coat conditioner, flea shampoo, tear stain remover, and a soft bristle cat brush. Don't buy rubber or wire "slicker" type brushes because they can damage the Himalayan's beautiful coat, and also slide over developing mats.

My tip: Buy good quality grooming supplies. Quality grooming supplies usually last for the life of your cat, and are well worth the money. Consult your breeder, groomer, or veterinarian for recommendations, or ask for advice at a well-stocked pet supply store or grooming distributor. Most necessary products can be found in pet supply stores, but some need to be purchased from a grooming supply store or from pet supply catalogs (see the mail-order list on page 102).

You can buy any number of products to keep your Himalayan from having a bad hair day. The same types of products sold for styling human hair are available for your cat's tresses, including dyes and hot oil treatments. Believe it or not, there's even a styling mousse made for cats to add body to

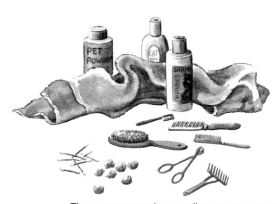

The proper grooming supplies are necessary to keep your Himalayan looking his best.

the fur, and it works essentially the same as it would on a human with long, fine hair. How many and which products you use depends upon the condition of the cat's coat and skin, your grooming enthusiasm, and your pocketbook. Will you be showing your Himalayan? That's an important consideration when choosing products.

Shampoos: Protein shampoos combat dryness, condition the coat, and build body. Tearless shampoos don't irritate the cat's eyes the way ordinary shampoos can and are recommended for Himalayans. Medicated shampoos relieve minor skin conditions such as dryness and flaking. If your cat has oily fur, degreasers help rid the coat of excessive oil, grease, and dirt. Herbal shampoos are available, as well as those containing oatmeal to soothe itchy skin, reduce static cling, and restore natural moisture. Coat brightening shampoos enhance the coat's color, and add brilliance and sparkle to the coat. Hypoallergenic shampoos are available for cats with sensitive skin. Finally, "dry" shampoos absorb the dirt and oils without water. These are good if your cat has a violent aversion to bathing.

Tick and flea shampoos, of course, kill parasites. Be sure parasites are actually present before you use these products, and be sure the label says "safe for cats." If the label does not, don't use the product on your cat as insecticide levels safe for dogs can be fatal to cats.

Rinses: Rinses untangle the coat, leaving it smooth, and add body. They also can cut down on static electricity in your pet's coat. Tangle removers loosen mats and make combing easier.

Coat conditioners: These products contain ingredients to condition, revitalize dry coats, add body, and aid manageability. Some contain lanolin to add luster and sheen.

Stain removers: If your Himalayan has a problem with excess tearing, a stain remover helps eliminate the tear stains under the eyes. These can also help remove urine and feces stains.

Nail Care

Trim your Himalayan's toenails every two to three weeks (unless, of course, you equip your cat with nail caps). Not only does nail trimming save on the furniture's wear and tear, it keeps the cat from hurting you and your other pets. Remember that an indoor cat's claws do not wear down as much as an outdoor cat's, and can grow into the paw's pad. Regular trimming prevents this.

Use nail clippers designed for cats or heavy-duty nail clippers designed for humans. With the cat held firmly in your lap, hold one paw and gently apply pressure. This makes the claws extend. Clip off the white part of the nail, being careful to avoid cutting the nail's pink "quick." The quick is rich with nerve endings and it is very painful if cut—probably akin to getting a sliver rammed under your fingernail. Don't cut the white part any closer than a tenth of an inch (2.5 cm) from the quick.

If you've never trimmed a cat's nails, ask your veterinarian or breeder to show you how. One experience with the "cruelest cut" and your Himalayan will hate the procedure from then on.

If the cat reacts badly, enlist an assistant's help to get the job done, or catch the cat just as he's waking from his afternoon nap. Be gentle and kind, and your cat will learn to accept nail trimming as just another incomprehensible thing humans do.

Eyes and Ears

The area around the eyes can accumulate dirt, dried tears, and sleep

Hold your Himalayan firmly in your lap and press the pad of the foot gently to extend the claws. Clip the white area of the nail. Be careful not to cut into the quick.

residue. Himalayans with a pronounced nose "break" (see Show Standard, page 8) can have narrow or blocked tear ducts that can cause excess tearing. Tearing leaves ugly yellowish-brown spots on the facial fur. During the weekly grooming session, or whenever the cat needs extra

To remove eye stains, gently wipe the area under the Himalayan's eyes with a cotton ball moistened with eye stain remover or warm water.

Flamepoint Himalayan. Immaculate facial grooming is important if your Himalayan will be competing in cat shows.

attention, wipe the eyes using a cotton ball moistened with warm (not hot) water. You can also use tear stain remover. Don't poke or scratch the eye or use any rough material, such as paper towels, that might injure the eye. If your Himalayan struggles, stop the procedure until he calms.

A normal, healthy cat's ears are clean and free of waxy discharge, and shouldn't require much attention. Look inside the inner flap. Clean off dirt and wax with a cotton ball or swab moistened with a few drops of olive oil. Clean the external ear only. Don't push into the ear canal because this can cause damage. If the ears show dark, waxy discharge, the cat probably has ear mites (see page 72).

Teeth

In the healthy adult Himalayan, the teeth are white and clean. The gums are firm and pink, and closely attached to the teeth. A bright red line along the gum near the teeth is a sign of gingivitis, or inflammation of the gums. Plaque deposits (a combination of bacteria, food particles, and saliva) harden onto tooth surfaces, and become tartar. The plaque and tartar enlarges the pocket between the tooth and the gum. These pockets become ideal homes for bacteria that invade the gingival tissue, causing swelling and bleeding. Eventually, the teeth loosen and fall out. When the gingivitis gets to this stage, the loose teeth must be removed and the remaining teeth cleaned in order for the inflammation to subside.

Spotting gingivitis is easy if you know what to look for. The classic signs are gum tenderness (your cat may cringe or flinch when you touch the side of his mouth), difficulty or pain when eating, drooling, and bad breath. The gums look red, inflamed, and swollen, and sometimes have small whitish ulcers that bleed when touched. If you see these symptoms, schedule an appointment with your veterinarian. If untreated, gingivitis can undermine your cat's health and affect his kidneys, nervous system, heart, and liver.

Cats can get cavities, too, developing tooth decay just under the gum line. The location makes it difficult to see the cavities. To prevent tooth loss, and to control tartar and gingivitis, brush your cat's teeth regularly.

My tip: Keeping your cat's teeth brushed extends the period between teeth cleanings, and that cuts down on the expense. Because cleaning a cat's teeth usually requires anesthesia, brushing his teeth yourself also cuts down on the risk. Discuss your cat's tooth care with your veterinarian and get his or her recommendation about the proper products and toothbrushing frequency.

Many veterinarians carry dental products or can recommend the proper items, and many pet supply stores carry dental products as well. Buy a toothbrush designed for cats, or a soft child's size toothbrush. Buy one brush for each cat to prevent transmitting bacteria. Diluted hydrogen peroxide works well to clean the teeth and gums, and is inexpensive, or you can buy a toothpaste designed for cats. Don't use human toothpaste because the foam frightens cats and the swallowed paste may cause stomach upset. You can also buy feline stannous fluoride products to help strengthen the enamel and inhibit plaque formation, and antibacterial gels to help reduce gum inflammation.

Brushing Your Cat's Teeth

Your Himalayan buddy won't like having his teeth brushed, particularly if his gums are sensitive or inflamed. Exercise patience and care. It's very important not to hurt your cat. You don't want to make your Himalayan dread the process and hide under the bed when the toothbrush comes out.

When you begin, limit the duration and talk to the cat encouragingly. It's helpful to have an assistant hold your cat while you brush.

Gently brush the tooth in a circular motion, and be very careful on the sensitive gums. It's usually not necessary to brush the inside tooth surfaces because the tongue cleans those. When finished, praise your cat warmly and give him a treat.

Coat Care

Unless your Himalayan is a show cat, he will do fine with a brief once-a-day combing and a thorough once-a-week grooming session. Additional grooming may be necessary during shedding months. Himalayans go through two shedding periods: in the spring when they shed their longer, heavier winter coats, and again in the fall before growing their winter coats.

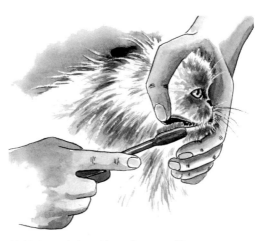

Hold the cat's head from the top, with your palm covering the top of the head. Gently pull back one corner of the mouth and insert the toothbrush between the teeth and the cheek. Brush the upper and lower teeth in a circular motion. Repeat on the other side.

HOW-TO:
Bathing Your Himalayan

Cats have an almost universal curiosity about water. They love to watch it, bat at it, and dabble their toes in it. Maybe this water fascination is the feline equivalent to our interest in horror movies; the fascination doesn't extend to actual emersion any more than we'd really want maniacs with chain saws chasing us.

Why Is Bathing Your Cat Necessary?

To keep your Himalayan looking her best, bathing is a necessity. Your indoor-only Himalayan won't need bathing as often as a cat who is allowed outdoors, but she'll still need regular bathing. Also, if your cat has chronic problems with parasites or skin allergies, or does not properly attend to her grooming, regular bathing certainly benefits her health. Obesity and pregnancy can make proper

grooming difficult for the Himalayan. Longhaired cats also have trouble keeping clean after a trip to the litter box.

Establish a routine early in the cat's life. Cats are creatures of habit. If you start bathing and grooming when your cat is young, she learns to tolerate these procedures much better than if you rarely bathe and groom her.

Where to Bathe Your Cat

You can bathe your cat in the bathtub, bathroom sink, or the kitchen sink. Many veterinarians recommend using a kitchen sink equipped with a spray hose attachment, because you have more control over the cat when you're standing up. You can buy an inexpensive rubber spray hose attachment at a bath supply store. If your sink is too small or the cat too big, use the tub. Whatever you choose, be sure you can close off the area. Chasing a wet, scared, soapy cat over the sofa and under the bed isn't much fun.

Before bathing your cat, trim her nails, and comb out the cat's fur thoroughly (see Grooming, page 52). *This last is very important.* Bathing "sets" mats into the hair. As the coat dries, the mats tighten up against the skin so they are impossible to remove and must be cut out with scissors.

Shampoo

You can use a flea-control shampoo (of course, only if your cat has fleas), a quality cat shampoo, or a gentle, protein-enriched shampoo designed for humans. Baby shampoo is fine. Mix the shampoo half and half with warm water in a plastic squeeze bottle with a valve top that can be closed. Diluting the shampoo makes it easier to work it into the coat and creates less suds, thereby making it easier to rinse out completely. However, don't dilute when using a flea shampoo.

How to Bathe

Run the bath water before you put the cat in. The sound of the water alarms cats. Keep the water at about the cat's normal body temperature of 101.4°F (38.5°C), or lower.

If you're bathing your cat in the tub, put two rectangular basins inside the tub and fill them with water, one for wetting the cat, the second for rinsing. If you're using a sink with two sides, fill one side only and use the hose attachment to rinse.

Put the cat into the sink or tub with her back facing you so she won't scratch you if she strikes out or struggles. Hold the cat in place by applying gentle pressure to the shoulders. If the

Hold the spray attachment close to the cat's body.

cat becomes uncontrollable, grip the nape and *push down*, being careful not to push the cat's head under water, which will cause panic. Gripping the nape makes the cat freeze because mother cats carry their young in this fashion. But never lift a full-grown cat by the nape—that can cause serious injury.

Wet the cat's coat thoroughly. Don't wet above the neckline, but if the cat has fleas, wet and shampoo the neck area first, keeping the fleas from escaping up the neck. If you're using a hose attachment, hold the hose close to the cat's body. This will scare the cat less than holding it farther away. Never spray the head, face, or ears, and *never* dunk a cat's head under water.

When the cat is completely wet, apply shampoo with the squeeze bottle. Work it into the coat well. Don't neglect the legs, feet, and tail, but be careful not to bend the tail tip. Put the cat into the first bucket again to rinse, or use the hose attachment. It's vital to get all the soap out of the fur, because your cat grooms after her bath and ingests any remaining soap. Continue rinsing until the fur has lost the slick, soapy feel and the rinse water runs off clear with no foaming action. Some Himalayan owners finish off their cat's bath with a hair rinse that removes tangles and leaves the coat smooth.

After rinsing her thoroughly, run your hands down her body to remove excess water and wrap her in a terry towel with just the head showing. Use a damp terry cloth washcloth to

The Himalayan's fur will look much better if it is blow-dried. Set the dryer on the lowest setting so you don't burn your cat.

clean head, face, and chin. Avoid getting soap in the eyes. Change the towel and dry the cat well. Pat, don't rub, the fur. That creates tangles. Change to a third towel if necessary.

Blow-drying Your Cat's Fur

After bathing your Himalayan you can allow her coat to air dry, but the hair will look much smoother and fluffier if you blow-dry it. The coat mats less, too. Most Himalayan owners blow-dry their cat's fur, and for the show Himalayan, it's essential. Whatever method you use, keep your cat warm and don't let her wander outside or into drafts. Chilling is good for white wine, not Himalayans.

The noise and sensation of the dryer frightens most cats. Begin training your Himalayan early to tolerate the noise. Bring the cat into the bathroom while blow-drying your own hair to show the cat that the dryer isn't dangerous. Use the blow dryer on the low setting only and avoid blowing directly into the cat's face or ears. Cats hate that.

Some Himalayan owners use their cat carrier as a drying cage. This allows them to dry their Himalayan without being required to hold the cat and the

dryer. Set up the dryer to blow into the carrier, and leave the Himalayan in the drying cage with the dryer set on low for about 20 minutes. Never leave the cat unattended with the dryer turned on.

After 20 minutes, take the cat from the drying cage and finish up the drying session. It helps to have an assistant, but if you don't, set up the dryer in its stand and direct the air stream at the section of fur on which you are working. Start at the hindquarters and work your way up to the neck. Comb against the lie, pulling the hairs up and away from the body to separate and aerate the fur. Stand the cat up and dry the belly and underarms, which helps prevent mats from forming and the belly hair from drying in unsightly little corkscrews.

After her bath, your Himalayan may pout, hide or pretend she doesn't remember who you are. Don't worry—just give her a special treat, tell her how beautiful she looks, and what a good cat she was—even if she wasn't. Eventually, your cat will forgive you. With persistence, gentleness, and love, your Himalayan may begin enjoying bath time—but don't count on it.

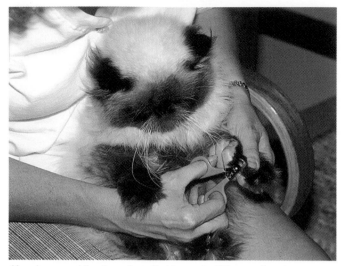
Keeping your Himalayan's nails trimmed will lessen the damage your pet can do to your furniture.

My tip: Try to make the once-a-day combing fun and stressless for you and your cat. After dinner, when you sit down to watch TV, take the cat onto your lap. Gently run the comb through his fur while giving him a cuddle. Or

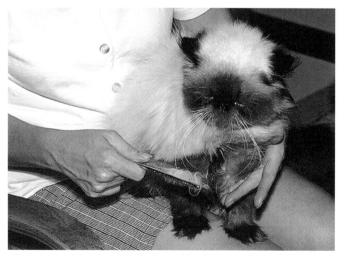
If you have difficulty grooming your Himalayan, ask your breeder for grooming tips. Breeders generally have years of experience grooming their cats.

you can groom your Himalayan in the bathroom while preparing for work or after you come home at night.

With their long, downy undercoats, Himalayans are prone to matting. These dense clumps of tangled hair often develop under the chin, behind the ears, under the arms, and on the tummy and britches. This can be a serious health concern. Mats form next to the skin, causing pain and damage if the mat is not combed out or clipped promptly. The pain can be extreme, and nothing makes cats hate grooming faster than the pain of their hair being pulled as the knots are combed out. Mats can also become nice, cozy condos for freeloading fleas and other parasites.

The Grooming Session

To begin the weekly grooming session, pick a spot such as the bathroom, back porch, or other enclosed area to make cleanup easier when your cat's fur flies. Before you take the cat to the grooming area, assemble all the grooming supplies. You don't want to run off to get something and come back to find that your Himalayan has wandered off or is hiding under the bed. I keep my grooming supplies in a plastic caddy, but any sturdy box would do to keep the supplies in one place and make transportation easy.

Run your hands over the cat's body, feeling for any swellings, lumps, growths, or abscesses. Check for tenderness, thin or bald spots, flea dirt, excessive skin flaking, and fur mats. Feel the tail gently for lumps, and the belly too, if your cat holds still for it. Some cats react negatively when you touch their tummies and may scratch or try to run away.

After you examine the cat, comb the fur thoroughly and gently with the lay of the fur, using a metal comb. Make sure you comb all the way down to the

Close association with humans has influenced the way cats react to their environment and to each other. However, cats still retain full use of their instincts.

skin. You can miss mats if you only comb the top layers. Pay particular attention to the underbelly and under-arms. Comb gently since these areas are sensitive. Snagging a mat with your comb can be very painful.

If, during this first gentle combing, you notice mats in your cat's fur, put a bit of cornstarch on the mat and then gently work the mat free with the tip of the comb or with a mat-breaker tool. Hold the hair clump against the cat's body with your other hand while you work on the mat so you won't pull on your cat's skin.

If the mat is particularly stubborn, try sliding the comb in between the skin and the mat and snipping the mat on the side of the comb away from the skin. Use a groomer's thinning shear,

and *be very careful.* A cat's skin is delicate, and it's easy to accidentally cut it, particularly if the cat wiggles at just the wrong moment. It only takes a painful snip or two for your Himalayan to hide under the bed when the cat comb comes out.

If your Himalayan becomes badly matted, let a professional groomer or veterinarian handle de-matting. The cat's coat may need to be shaved. *Don't try this at home.*

After removing the mats, comb the fur starting at the head and work down to the tail, combing with the coat's lie. "Backcombing" (combing against the lie) the flank, neck, and tail gives your Himalayan a fuller look. Hold the tail's tip and gently comb down the tail's length to fluff it like a bottle brush.

Your Himalayan's fur must be combed often to prevent the formation of painful and damaging mats.

Finally, comb the ruff forward to frame the face.

Comb gently and talk softly. Many Himalayans like combing. Mother cats groom their kittens, and since your cat sees you as a surrogate "cat-mom" or "cat-dad," your cat should tolerate grooming without too much protest.

If the cat tries to run away or behaves aggressively, limit the grooming session to a few minutes and slowly work up to longer sessions. Maybe you're being too rough. As you comb, watch the cat's body language. If the cat flattens his ears and lashes his tail, he's becoming angry. Take a break for a while, and return later when your cat has calmed. Save the procedures your cat dislikes—such as nail clipping or bathing—for a separate grooming session, so he doesn't associate his general grooming with these unpleasant activities.

If you suspect the cat has a problem with fleas, comb the coat with a fine-toothed "flea comb," which catches fleas and flea wastes in its narrow teeth. First set the cat on a light-colored towel so you can see any fleas or debris. If you see fleas or flea wastes, decide on a course of treatment right away (see Parasites, page 72).

After grooming, treat your Himalayan to a weekly dose of a petrolatum product such as Kittymalt or Petromalt to help prevent hairballs. To administer, smear a dab onto the paw and allow the cat to lick it off. (The cat picks up less fur if you dispense this after grooming.) I recommend using a hairball preventive for the longhaired Himalayan. Use only as directed. Too much of the product can hinder the absorption of fat-soluble vitamins.

Nutrition and Feeding

You are what you eat—and that's true for cats as well as humans. As it is for all of us, proper nutrition is vital for a Himalayan to live a long and healthy life. Dietary needs vary depending upon the life stage: growth, adult maintenance, pregnancy, or the senior years. Requirements also vary depending upon the cat's activity level and metabolic rate.

Dietary Needs

Cats are descended from the African Wildcat, a desert animal, and the cat's physiology is designed for survival in that harsh environment by consuming prey animals. In the wild, cats get all the nutrients they need from the muscle, bones, and organs of their prey, including most of their water intake, and essential chemicals such as taurine that their bodies cannot manufacture but their prey's bodies can. Cats are true metabolic carnivores. Their metabolism is designed to derive all needed nutrients from animal sources.

The cat's digestive tract is relatively short, and therefore cats need easily digestible foods to supply their nutritional needs. The essential elements of a cat's diet are protein, fats, vitamins, minerals, and water. Carbohydrates are commonly added to cat food as well.

Protein: Food provides the energy we use to do all the things life requires of us. Protein (along with fats and carbohydrates) provides energy. Protein is also vital to maintain the body's functions and to replace the body's tissues. In general, a cat's diet should consist of 30 to 40 percent protein derived from animal sources such as eggs, meat, offal, fish, and milk.

The amino acids needed to synthesize the body's proteins are divided into two groups: dispensable, and indispensable. Dispensable amino acids are those the cat synthesizes in the liver. Indispensable are those the cat's body must have but doesn't manufacture. The diet must provide indispensable amino acids for the cat to remain healthy.

Cats require two to three times more protein than dogs do. For that reason, don't feed a cat dog food. It's not high enough in protein to satisfy a cat's needs.

Fats: Fats are vital nutrients, and a concentrated energy source. Fat is needed for absorption of fat-soluble vitamins. It makes the cat's food taste good, too. However, too much fat, just

Your Himalayan requires a balanced diet in order to stay healthy. Be sure to read the pet food label to be sure your cat is getting the nutrients she needs.

The safest and most convenient way to be sure your pampered house pet gets the nutrition he needs is to feed a good quality commercial cat food.

as with humans, can make a cat pudgy. Monitor your cat's fat intake.

Cats can digest fat more easily than humans can, and so fat should comprise about 25 to 30 percent of the cat's caloric intake, or about 8 to 10 percent of the food by weight. Most quality cat foods provide the proper balance of nutrients.

Essential fatty acids: These are vital to maintaining the cat's skin integrity, membrane function, and reproduction. Cats must receive these fatty acids from animal fats.

Vitamins: Vitamins are either fat soluble or water soluble. Fat soluble vitamins such as A, D, E, and K are stored in the body. Water soluble vitamins such as B-complex must be replenished daily through food sources, since they pass quickly from the body. (Vitamin C is also water soluble, but the cat's liver synthesizes it in adequate amounts.)

Vitamins help maintain body processes such as the immune system, red blood cell formation, and bone metabolism. They are also essential for the enzyme system's functioning. Shortage of essential vitamins can cause dietary diseases. However, some vitamins, such as A and D, are toxic in large amounts. Vitamin A overdose causes swollen, painful joints (similar to the symptoms of vitamin A deficiency). Vitamin supplements are usually not necessary if you're feeding your cat a good brand of cat food.

Minerals: Minerals are divided into two groups: macrominerals

Blue-cream point Himalayan. Blue-cream is a variety of Tortoiseshell.

(calcium, phosphorus, magnesium, potassium, sodium, and chloride) and microminerals (iron, copper, iodine, zinc, manganese, and selenium). These are necessary for the body's functioning and for bone and tissue development, to maintain electrolyte and acid-base balance, and to aid in nerve cell function. A complete cat food should provide all necessary minerals.

Water: Since cats are the descendants of desert animals, their bodies can concentrate urine to high levels, and retain water if availability is restricted. In the wild, cats can derive most of the water they need from their prey. If you're feeding your cat canned food, she can derive most of the water she needs from the food. However,

Body posture tells a lot about the attitude and health of the cat. This cat is obviously healthy and happy.

water is vital to almost every body system, so your pampered house pet always needs a fresh supply. Each day, cats need about one fluid ounce (30 mL) of water for every pound (0.5 kg) of body weight. Provide your cat with a bowl of water and freshen it as needed. Clean the bowl well at least once a week.

Carbohydrates: A cat's body doesn't require carbohydrates such as starches and sugars, but these add energy and roughage, and are included in most commercial cat foods. Common carbohydrates used are rice, corn, and soybeans.

Stages of Life

A good quality cat food should provide all the elements a cat needs. Since nutritional needs are different at the various life stages, adjust the food you give your cats according to their age range.

Kittens: A kitten should receive a good quality kitten food for the first 12 months of life. Because they are busy growing, kittens need more protein. Kitten food is formulated to provide the nutrients a kitten needs to grow. It must be 35 to 40 percent protein, and about 17 percent fat.

Adult Himalayans: Since an adult Himalayan needs a well-balanced and complete diet to remain healthy, provide a good quality cat food designed for adult cats. Don't rely on meat scraps, tuna, or kitty treats. A combination of canned and dry food is a good choice. The cat benefits from the canned food's protein and moisture content, while still receiving the dry's tarter-controlling benefit. Buy the best quality food you can, because a complete and balanced diet today means fewer health problems and vet bills tomorrow.

Pregnant cats: Pregnant queens require about 25 percent more protein than adult cats. The energy needs of lactating Himalayan queens are two to four times higher than for non-pregnant adult cats. To ensure proper nutrition, feed a pregnant Himalayan a high protein food, available at pet supply stores or from your veterinarian.

The senior years: Senior cats are less active and have a lower rate of metabolism. Therefore, their energy needs are less. The National Research Council recommends feeding senior cats 32 calories per pound (0.5 kg) of body weight per day. Senior cats with a tendency toward obesity need a low calorie diet (see Obesity, page 75).

Types of Cat Foods

Three types are available: dry, semimoist, and canned. Each has advantages and disadvantages.

Dry foods consist of animal protein meals, cereals, corn and soy meal, and supplements, formed into small, crunchy, fat-covered nuggets. Dry food is inexpensive and easy to store, since it doesn't go bad as quickly as canned or semimoist foods. The chewing action also reduces tartar buildup on the cat's teeth, and helps maintain healthy teeth and gums.

However, studies show that cats eating dry food exclusively have a six to seven times greater risk of developing Lower Urinary Tract Disease (LUTD), a potentially life-threatening condition. This is attributed to the higher magnesium content in dry food. Also, when food is available for continuous snacking, the cat's urine pH becomes alkaline, providing favorable conditions for the formulation of the urinary crystals that block the urethra. If you're going to feed your cat dry food, keep the feeding schedule consistent. Because the Himalayan and the closely related Persian are at higher risk for this disorder, don't feed your cat solely dry food (see Health Care, page 68).

Semimoist foods have a higher moisture content than dry foods but are produced in much the same way and have the same ingredients. They have the same advantages in that they are easy to store and lower in cost than canned foods. Your cat may also find them more palatable than dry foods.

The primary difference between dry and semimoist is that semimoist has chemical preservative additives such as propylene glycol to prevent spoiling. The effects of these chemicals on felines has not been completely established, although in some studies they have been linked with oxidative damage to the red blood cells. Also, semimoist foods won't keep the teeth tartar free, so a combination of semimoist and dry foods is advisable.

Canned foods are slightly more expensive than the other two and not as easy to store, but they are highly digestible, higher in protein, and your Himalayan may like them better than dry or semimoist, making them good choices for finicky eaters. Canned foods are about 75 percent water and are a good source for cats that need a higher fluid intake, such as those with renal disease. Cover and refrigerate leftover canned food.

My tip: Whatever type of food you decide on, avoid feeding your cat only one flavor of food exclusively. An exclusive diet of some foods can cause dietary diseases. For example, a fish diet (such as tuna) can lead to vitamin E deficiency. Cats need variety in order to get complete nutrition. If you're feeding your cat a good quality, complete cat food, supplements are usually not necessary.

Pet Food Labels

These days it pays to be an informed consumer. To insure proper nutrition for your Himalayan, know what to look for when reading a cat food label. Even some higher priced foods are not nutritionally complete, and if fed to a cat over a long period,

The "catnip response" has been noted in wild cats as well as domestics. Lions, cougars, and leopards react to catnip in the same way as your Himalayan does—by sniffing, chewing, rubbing, rolling, and meowing.

could result in nutritional disorders and diseases.

Pet food manufacturers must supply certain nutritional information on the label. The rules governing pet food labels are based on Model Pet Food Regulations set by the Association of American Feed Control Officials (AAFCO) to ensure compliance with federal and state feed regulations. The label must disclose the following:

Guaranteed analysis: This specifies the minimum amounts of protein and fat, and the maximum amounts of fiber and moisture. The analysis may also list maximums and minimums of ash, magnesium, and taurine, among other nutrients. The word "crude" when applied to the protein, fat, and fiber percentages does not refer to the quality of those items. It describes the method used to determine the percentage. "Crude" means the percentage is an estimate.

The protein percentage listed on the label means the food contains at least that amount of protein. However, that doesn't explain how much of the

Cats who carry the colorpoint gene but look like Persians are called Colorpoint Carriers. If bred to cats who also possess the colorpoint gene, Himalayan offspring can result.

A pot of oat grass will satisfy your indoor Himalayan's desire to "graze."

Adult cats can seem like kittens again when under the influence of catnip.

percentage's total is the animal protein the cat requires, and how much is vegetable protein. These percentages can fool you into thinking the cat is getting more useable protein than she really is.

Ingredients list: This list must disclose all the items used in the food. Just as in human foods, the ingredients are listed in decreasing order by weight. You get an indication of the amount of any item by where it appears in the order. Therefore, to determine how much animal protein your cat is getting, see where meat products fall *in order* in the ingredients list.

Statement of nutritional adequacy: This tells whether or not the food provides complete nutrition for cats, and for what life stage(s). The label will say something like this: *This food provides complete and balanced nutrition for all life stages as substantiated by feeding tests using AAFCO procedures.*

When examining this statement on your brand of cat food, note whether or not the words *complete and balanced* appear, whether the food has undergone feeding tests, and for what

life stage the food is designed. You want a food that has been test fed to cats with the procedures established by AAFCO, and guarantees complete nutrition for your cat's current stage of life (kitten, growth, adult maintenance, pregnancy, senior, or all stages). If the food label says "for intermittent feeding only" or "use as snack," the food doesn't provide complete nutrition for any life stage.

Flavor classifications: If the label reads "tuna flavor," the food has only a very small amount of real tuna. It's just *flavored* with tuna. If the label says it's "tuna supper," "tuna meal," or words to that effect, the food has to have 10 percent tuna. If, however, it says it's "tuna cat food," it must have at least 70 percent real tuna. A cat food claiming to be 100 percent of one type of food wouldn't provide a balanced diet, since it then couldn't have added supplements.

Feeding instructions: Most cat food labels provide feeding instructions. The instructions say something like this, "An average 8 to 10 pound (4–5 kg) adult cat eats about two

3-ounce (100 g) cans per day when fed this food exclusively." Or it might say, "The daily ration for an average adult cat is one 3-ounce (100 g) can per 3 pounds (1.5 g) of body weight."

My tip: Many cat food labels give you the company's phone number (often an 800 number) or address in case you have questions or problems. Call these numbers and ask if they can provide you with coupons to use with their products. They also may give you information about the product's nutrition and feeding trial results.

Treats

It's okay to give your Himalayan an occasional treat. We all need a special goody now and then. Also, treats can be excellent training tools when you're teaching your cat to, say, hold still for her weekly grooming session. *Occasional* is the significant word here, because too many treats can lead to finicky eating and, as with human kids, can spoil your cat's appetite for supper. Because most commercial cat treats are not nutritionally complete, don't use them in place of regular meals.

An occasional milk treat is acceptable, unless the cat is lactose sensitive. Intolerance to the milk sugar lactose can cause diarrhea or flatulence. If your cat displays these symptoms, avoid milk products.

Never feed your Himalayan raw meat, fish, or eggs as a treat (or as a meal either), because of the risk of developing toxoplasma tissue cysts, which can lead to the disease toxoplasmosis. Raw meat can also contain parasites such as Trichinella spiralis, which causes the disease trichinosis. Raw eggs can carry the salmonella bacteria. Raw egg whites contain a substance that destroys the B vitamin biotin.

Catnip

Catnip (*Nepeta cataria*, also called *catmint*), is a perennial herb with pale green triangular leaves that feel like soft velvet. In the summer the stalks sprout purple and white flowers that in turn produce tiny brown seeds. Catnip has a spicy, refreshing scent. Catnip leaves and stems are often used in cat toys to increase interest.

Catnip contains a chemical called *nepetalactone*, which causes the cat's euphoric reaction. The effects seem psychotropic (mind altering), based on the behavior of cats that have taken "a nip." Catnip does not appear to be addictive or harmful to cats; however, use it in moderation because your cat can become desensitized to its effects. Two or three times a month is fine.

Typical reactions of both wild and domestic cats include euphoric rolling, rubbing, and sleeping. The reactions can resemble the queen's estrus behavior. However, catnip is not considered a feline aphrodisiac.

Although 30 percent of domestic cats lack the catnip gene and couldn't care less about "nipping," the other 70 percent enjoy it in varying degrees. Some react mildly and some go wild over the plant. The volatile chemicals are concentrated when the leaves are dried, and produces a stronger reaction than the fresh leaves do.

Health Care and Diseases

A healthy cat is sleek, happy, and active. Her nose is cool and slightly damp, her eyes bright and without excessive tearing, and her fur clean and shiny. Her nose doesn't run, her breathing is quiet, and her breath sweet. The ears are clean and free of wax, and her gums are pink rather than pale or red and inflamed.

A healthy Himalayan sleeps—a lot! Himalayans sleep 16 to 18 hours a day. Usually, a normal, healthy Himalayan has an active period in the morning, then sleeps throughout the afternoon, and becomes active again in the evening around dinnertime, or later when you're trying to sleep.

Serious Symptoms

If you see any of the following signs, take the cat to the veterinarian immediately:
• abdominal pain/body held in a hunched position
• bleeding/abnormal discharge from a body opening
• coat changes (dullness, dandruff, excessive shedding, loss of hair, bald patches)
• difficult urination, inability to urinate, blood in the urine
• difficulty in breathing; wheezing, choking
• discolored tongue
• disorientation
• extreme thirst, increased water intake
• increased hunger or food intake
• increased urination
• lumps or swellings
• persistent cough
• pupils different sizes or unresponsive to light
• refusal to eat or drink
• repeated vomiting
• seizures
• severe diarrhea
• staggering, head tilt, inability to walk normally
• sudden blindness or vision disturbances
• unexplained weight loss or gain
• unresponsiveness, unconsciousness, extreme languor, weakness

Vaccinations

Proper vaccination can prevent some of the most common and dangerous feline diseases. While no vaccination is 100 percent effective, vaccinations have saved countless feline lives. It's up to cat owners to keep debilitating and deadly feline diseases at bay. Make yearly vaccinations part of your cat's basic health care.

Vaccinations work by introducing a modified form of the disease into the cat's system, causing the cat's body to develop antibodies against the disease organisms. This usually results in immunity. Although vaccines are usually safe and adverse effects are rare, occasionally life-threatening systemic reactions can occur. Because of possible complications, only qualified veterinary personnel should administer vaccinations. See the vaccination chart on page 65 for the intervals.

Vaccinations are particularly important if your cat goes outside, even for

Most vaccinations should be started when a kitten is eight to ten weeks old.

A healthy Himalayan has clear eyes and a shiny coat.

short periods and under supervision. Cats can be quickly exposed to disease transmitters, such as other cats and their wastes, parasites, and wildlife. Have the yearly vaccinations done whether you intend to let the cat outside or not. You never know when a cat may make a break for the great outdoors, and some states require vaccination against some diseases such as rabies.

Diseases and Illnesses

Whether you buy a Himalayan or pick up an alley cat, you will likely become familiar with certain feline disorders over the course of your relationship with your furry feline friend. The following is a short course in some of the common ailments and diseases, symptoms, and treatment options. Some are preventable with proper vaccination.

Feline Infectious Peritonitis (FIP)

The disease associated with the FIP virus is actually caused by the body's immune response to the virus. The immune response assists the virus to spread throughout the body and cause damage. Researchers think

Yearly vaccinations will help keep your Himalayan happy and healthy.

Recommended Vaccinations

Disease	Type Vaccination	1st Vaccination	2nd Vaccination	Revaccination
Panleukopenia	Inactivated, MLV, MLV-IN	8–10 weeks	12–14 weeks	yearly
Caliciviruses	Inactivated, MLV, MLV-IN	8–10 weeks	12–14 weeks	yearly
Rhinotracheitis	Inactivated, MLV, MLV-IN	8–10 weeks	12–14 weeks	yearly
Rabies	Inactivated	12 weeks	64 weeks	tri-annually
FeLV (Leukemia)	Inactivated	9 weeks	12 weeks	yearly
Chlamydiosis	Live Attenuated	8–10 weeks	12–14 weeks	yearly
FIP (Infectious peritonitis)	MLV	16 weeks	18 weeks	yearly

this virus is transmitted through bodily secretions such as feces or saliva, and contaminated objects such as dishes and litter boxes.

Two forms of the disease exist. The "wet" form is characterized by fluid accumulation within a cat's abdomen or chest that results in laborious breathing. Other symptoms include fever, listlessness, and appetite and weight loss. Usually the cat lives only days or weeks after the initial signs appear.

The "dry" form progresses more slowly. Symptoms vary, depending on the body areas affected, but usually include lethargy, weight loss, and intermittent fever. A cat with the dry form usually dies within weeks or months of getting the disease.

FIP is usually fatal; no known effective treatment or cure exists. Fortunately, an effective and safe intranasal vaccine for FIP is available (see page 65).

Feline Leukemia Virus (FeLV)

FeLV attacks the body three ways: by causing tumors, by attacking the growing blood cells in the bone marrow, and by suppressing the immune system. One of the chief symptoms is rapid weight loss. Also watch for symptoms such as sluggishness, poor appetite, and recurring colds and infections. Once the symptoms appear, the cat usually dies within three months to three years. However, a cat can go months or years carrying the dormant FeLV virus, appearing completely healthy.

Common modes of transmission are through saliva and respiratory secretions, particularly through activities such as mutual grooming, eating from the same bowl, sharing a litter box, or biting wounds.

Fighting FeLV involves three important steps: testing, vaccinating, and isolating infected cats. It's necessary to test for FeLV before vaccination as vaccination won't help an infected cat and the cat continues to spread the disease after being vaccinated. It is essential to vaccinate indoor-outdoor cats, or cats having contact with other felines, such as show cats.

Feline Immune Deficiency Virus (FIV)

FIV is a newly recognized feline virus resulting in *immunosuppression*— it suppresses the feline's normal immune response. The cat may appear completely healthy for months or years after infection. Eventually, the signs begin to appear as the disease suppresses the immune system's response, allowing secondary infections to take hold. Although this disease is similar to AIDS in humans, rest assured that FIV is species-specific. Contrary to recent erroneous rumors, *it does not cause human AIDS and poses no threat to humans or non-feline companion animals.* Nor can cats get AIDS from humans.

The common mode of transmission is bite wounds. Like human AIDS, casual contact among cats is not an efficient way to transmit the disease. You can keep a FIV-infected cat in a multi-cat environment with little risk to the uninfected cats, if they are well socialized.

Because the symptoms of the secondary infections vary, FIV is hard to identify and is easily confused with FeLV. Treatment options include protecting the cat from infections, and treating the secondary infections when and if they occur. No cure or vaccines are currently available for FIV, but research is underway. The best prevention is to keep the cat away from high-risk cats (free-roaming, unneutered males). Any new cat brought into the household should be tested.

Feline Panleukopenia Virus (FPV, Feline Distemper)

Panleukopenia is one of the most contagious and destructive feline diseases. The virus is transmitted by direct contact with an infected cat's feces, urine, saliva, vomitus, or fleas, and indirectly from contact with contaminated objects. You can also bring the virus home if you touch an infected cat, or step in an infected cat's excrement or bodily fluid.

Onset is sudden and is characterized by any or all of these symptoms: fever, appetite loss, dehydration, depression, coat dullness, vomiting, and abdominal pain. Infected cats often assume a hunched position. The mortality rate for this disease is high. The best defense is vaccination.

Rabies

Rabies (hydrophobia) is probably the best known and most feared zoonotic disease, and for good reason. Once the clinical signs manifest, the mortality rate is virtually 100 percent. This disease can infect warm-blooded animals such as cats, dogs, bats, skunks, foxes, raccoons, and humans.

The rabies virus is secreted in vast numbers in the infected animal's saliva, which makes bite wounds the primary means of transmission.

The animal may first become withdrawn and hide. In a few days, she becomes irritable and attacks anyone within reach. Infected animals also may seem deranged and try to bite imaginary objects.

Even with your Himalayan cat always indoors, keep her rabies vaccination current. Don't take the chance.

Respiratory Ailments

Cats are susceptible to viral infections called upper respiratory infections, or the "Cat Flu." Symptoms include sneezing, noisy or labored breathing, coughing, and nasal discharge. Take these symptoms seriously, because the infections can be life threatening, and can also indicate other diseases or conditions. See your veterinarian and be prepared to participate in the cat's convalescence (see HOW-TO, page 70).

FVR, FCV, and other cat respiratory diseases spread easily, particularly in catteries. Even after the cat has recovered from the disease and is no longer symptomatic, she carries the disease and can transmit it to other cats.

Feline Viral Rhinotracheitis

Also called FVR, rhino, and feline herpes, this acute disease affects the respiratory system. Symptoms are similar to our common cold, and include sneezing and coughing. Next the eyes become red, swollen, and sensitive to light. The eyes produce a watery discharge, and the nose usually runs and forms a crust. Fever may be present, and the cat may seem depressed and may stop eating.

Like the cold virus, FVR transmits easily from one cat to another through direct contact, shared feeding and water dishes, litter pans, or aerosol droplets drifting in the air from the emissions of an infected cat. Humans caring for infected cats can carry FVR on the hands, clothes, or feet. The risk of infecting your cat by petting a strange cat is small, although washing your hands after handling an unfamiliar animal is a wise habit to develop.

Treatment for FVR is usually symptomatic. Antibiotics are given to treat secondary infections. In severe cases, fluids are given to overcome dehydration, and oxygen is given if lack of respiratory function decreases the cat's oxygen intake.

Caliciviruses (FCV)

This respiratory disease is similar to FVR, but the infection is usually

Sealpoint Himalayan. The length and density of the Himalayan's coat changes with the seasons. In the winter, the coat is thicker and heavier.

milder. However, FCV can cause pneumonia which can be fatal, particularly to young kittens. Treatment is the same as for FVR. Vaccination is available for this disease.

Lower Urinary Tract Disease

Formerly called FUS, Lower Urinary Tract Disease (LUTD) is a group of disorders and diseases affecting the urinary tract and can be caused by a variety of factors including bacteria, fungus, parasites, anatomic abnormalities, and tumors. Cats with LUTD develop sand size crystals in their urine, which, combined with mucus and sloughed tissue and blood, can form blockages in the urinary tract. Persians have a higher than average risk of developing this disorder, which means the closely related Himalayan is also at high risk. Research also shows that less active cats and obese cats may be at higher risk. Too much magnesium and phosphorus in a cat's diet can contribute to forming crystals, so a cat food low in these minerals is recommended for the Himalayan (see Nutrition, page 58).

Blockages occur more frequently in male cats than in females. Symptoms of LUTD include inappropriate urination, frequent voiding, straining at the end of urination, and blood in the urine. The cat also may be off her feed and excessively thirsty. If the cat strains to urinate and produces only a tiny amount of urine, take her to the vet immediately. This is a life-threatening emergency.

Hairballs

Hairballs are small dense elongated bits of swallowed hair that accumulate in a cat's stomach. Even short-haired breeds are susceptible, but Himalayans, with their long, luxurious fur, are particularly predisposed. Cats groom themselves continually, and their tongues are like miniature rasps perfect for gathering hair that they swallow during the grooming process.

Tortiepoint Himalayan. A blaze of red on the face is a desirable attribute for the Tortiepoint Himalayan.

Usually the hair moves through the digestive tract and passes out with the feces with no trouble. Sometimes, however, the hair accumulates in the stomach, forming compact balls. Usually the cat vomits them up onto your newly cleaned rug. This is a normal process for cats as their systems are designed to rid themselves of indigestible items such as feathers (for example). Hairballs are not a cause for concern as long as they are occasional (except you now have to get out the rug cleaner). You should be aware, however, that hairballs lead to constipation, or even life-threatening obstructions. Symptoms include vomiting, appetite loss, wheezing, retching, and a swollen and painful abdomen. If your cat displays any of these symptoms, take her to the veterinarian immediately.

My tip: Regular grooming helps cut down on swallowed hair. Petrolatum products also help (see Grooming, page 54). A high-fiber diet helps elimi-nate constipation (no pun intended), and helps the hair pass through the cat's system.

Eye Ailments

Because of the foreshortened muzzle, Himalayans and Persians can have constrictions or blocks in the ducts that drain tears into the nasal cavity. This causes tears to overflow at the inner corners of the eyes. The tears leave yellow or brown stains on the facial fur. This isn't really cause for concern, unless you wish to show your Himalayan (see Grooming, page 47). Ask your veterinarian if he or she can prescribe eye drops to reduce the tearing.

The Siamese "squint" is a genetic disorder that causes abnormal nerve connections between the eye and brain, resulting in double vision. The cat squints in an attempt to correct this. Since the Himalayan is a product of a Siamese/Persian cross, this gene can crop up in the Himalayan,

69

HOW-TO:
Caring for Your Sick Himalayan

Cats sometimes need to be nursed back to health, just like humans do. It's important to know how to care for your Himalayan at home after the veterinarian has diagnosed the problem and outlined a course of treatment.

Medicating Your Cat

Medicating your cat can be a wild ride if you've never done it before. Patience and praise are important to make this task tolerable for all concerned. Medications can come in several forms: pills, liquids, pastes, and ointments. If your cat struggles wildly, use the restraining methods outlined in the first aid section beginning on page 77.

Administering Pills and Tablets

Open your cat's mouth and drop the pill as far back in the

Gently pry open the cat's mouth and tilt the head back. Drop the pill as far back in the mouth as possible. Gently hold the cat's mouth closed until she has swallowed.

mouth as possible to get it past the back of the tongue. Then hold your cat's mouth closed and stroke the throat gently to encourage him to swallow, while praising his exemplary behavior. The first few times, your cat may react very strongly, because he doesn't understand what you're doing. Given time, he will learn that you're not trying to hurt him, and will swallow the pills without too much protest. Do not crush the pills to aid administration without first checking with your veterinarian.

It is useful to have an assistant help hold the cat while you give the medication. If the pill is large, you can smear the pill with butter to help it slide down more easily. You can tell the pill has been swallowed if the cat licks his nose.

Administering Liquids

Give liquid medications with an eye dropper or syringe (without the needle attached). Administer the liquid 2 to 3 drops at a time into the cat's mouth. Allow the cat to swallow before giving more.

You can also try mixing the medication in a *small amount* of your cat's favorite food; however, some medications are too bitter for this to be effective. Be sure the cat eats all of the medicated treat, and that your other cats do not share the food. Talk to your veterinarian before attempting this technique, because this method is not appropriate for all types of medication.

Administering Pastes

Pastes, such as hairball med-

ication, are made to be palatable to cats. Some cats will lick the medication off your finger if you act like it's a treat you're offering and don't first try to shove the medication down your cat's throat. If you're not that lucky, you can either use the "pilling" method or, if the medication is not too bitter, you can wipe the paste onto the cat's paw. The cat licks it off and swallows it.

Administering Ointments

Veterinarians prescribe external ointments for various skin conditions. Rub the ointment into the affected area thoroughly. Keep your cat from licking the area for at least 15 minutes. Put an Elizabethan collar on your cat, or hold him. You can also try to distract your cat by feeding, grooming, or playing with him. Some ointments are intentionally bitter to discourage cats from licking them off. Consult your veterinarian.

Administering Injections

Trained veterinary personnel usually administer injections. However, some diseases, such as feline diabetes, require regular injections your veterinarian can train you to give at home. Ask your veterinarian to instruct you before you attempt to give your cat an injection.

Applying Ointment to a Cat's Eyes

Himalayans typically do not look forward to this treatment, but it's important to apply the medication as the veterinarian instructs. Conjunctivitis (see page 72) and certain other con-

Hold the cat's head steady. Be sure you don't poke your Himalayan's eye as you apply the medication.

ditions require the application of eye ointment. Restrain your Himalayan by using the towel technique (see page 51), or by wedging the cat between your knees with the cat facing outward. An assistant is also helpful. Tilt the cat's head up slightly. Keep the tube of medication parallel to the eye, and gently squeeze a line of ointment onto the eyeball. Be careful not to poke your Himalayan's eye. If he struggles, stop and wait for him to calm before trying again. Hold the eye closed for a few moments by pushing gently up on the cheek; this will give the medication time to melt onto the surface of the eye.

Instilling Ear Drops

Various conditions such as ear mites and infections require medication to be applied to the inside of the ear. Have an assistant hold the cat while you drop the prescribed number of drops into the affected ear

canal, being careful not to poke the applicator into the ear canal. Massage the ear gently to spread the medication.

Taking a Cat's Temperature

Taking a cat's temperature helps you determine whether your Himalayan is sick or just feeling grouchy today. A healthy cat's temperature is 100 to 102.5°F (37.8–39°C). If your cat's temperature is 105°F (40.6°C), take him to the veterinarian right away.

Use a human rectal thermometer (not an oral one), and shake it down to 96°F (35.6°C) or lower, then lubricate it with KY Jelly or petroleum gel. Have an assistant gently hold the cat by placing one restraining hand on the chest and the other hand on the scruff. While the cat is being held, lift the cat's tail and slowly insert the thermometer into the anus until about an inch (2.5 cm) of the thermometer is inside the cat. Leave it in place for one to two minutes, then remove and read. *Never* attempt to read a cat's temperature orally; if the cat bites down, the thermometer will shatter.

Feeding a Sick Himalayan

Eating and drinking are important to your cat's recovery. You may have to help your cat when he is ill, because cats who feel poorly are often off their feed. Feeding your cat pungent fish such as tuna may help. Try adding the water or oil from canned tuna to your cat's food.

It's a good idea to have your veterinarian show you how to take your cat's temperature before you attempt it for the first time.

This also works when trying to induce your cat to take fluids.

Smell is also very important to a cat's feeding habits, so a congested cat may eat less or not at all. Cleaning the nose of nasal discharge with a cotton ball moistened with water may help.

Paste and Liquid Foods

If all else fails, a variety of paste and liquid foods are available at pet supply stores and your vet's office. Give paste foods by holding your cat in the "pilling position." Tip the head up slightly, hold the mouth open, and place a strip of paste into the mouth. The cat usually attempts to swallow. Do not release the head because the cat may spit out the food or shake his head, spraying food everywhere.

Some diseases cause your cat to become dehydrated and your veterinarian may suggest administering water. You can give liquid foods or water by using the same method used to give liquid medication.

71

Blue-creampoint Himalayan. Blue-cream is a genetic "dilute" version of Tortoiseshell.

develop on the surface of the cornea. This condition is seen most often in Persian and Himalayan cats. It is treated with veterinarian-prescribed medication, and sometimes a soft contact lens is put over the eye to help it heal.

Ear Problems

Ear problems in cats are usually due to parasites or injury. Another cat's claws can cause lacerations, but the ears can also be injured from a cat's attempts to ease an itch or irritation. If your cat shakes her head or scratches at her ears, or if you see dark brown, waxy deposits in the cat's ears, it's usually a sign of parasitic infestation (see ear mites, page 73), ear infection, or a foreign body in the ear, such as a foxtail. Foxtails are a particular problem to the Himalayan, because they cling to the long hair. Don't ignore these symptoms. See your veterinarian.

Parasites

Everyone has to make a living, and parasites make theirs at the expense of your cat. Parasites ingest the cat's blood, cells, and tissues, undermining the cat's health and sometimes transmitting dangerous organisms as well. Parasites are divided into two groups: external and internal.

External parasites: External parasites, such as fleas, ticks, flies, lice, and some mites, live on the skin, in the ears, and in the hair of cats. Long, matted hair makes excellent hiding places for parasites, and that's another reason to keep up with your Himalayan's grooming.

Mites: Mites are microscopic organisms living on or in cats' skin or in their hair. Symptoms (collectively called *mange*) include bald patches, dandruff, dermatitis, skin crust, and lesions. Mites are contagious and are transmitted by bedding and grooming equipment.

although selective breeding has largely eliminated the problem.

Conjunctivitis, inflammation of the eyelid membranes, is a common ailment in cats, and can be caused by several factors: injury, bacteria, viruses, plant pollens, and irritants such as cigarette smoke. Symptoms include blinking, cloudy or discolored discharge from the eye, and reddened, exposed, or swollen third eyelids (also called *haws* or *nictating membranes*). Don't hesitate—it's time to visit the veterinarian. He or she can prescribe ointments to help the eye heal.

If you notice brown or black spots on the surface of your cat's cornea, take the cat to see the veterinarian. It could be a sign of *corneal sequestration*, where deposits of pigment

Ear mites live inside the ear canal and suck blood from the wall of the ear to survive. You'll notice an unpleasant smell and a dark discharge that looks like coffee grounds in the ear. If not treated, ear mites and infections can cause disfiguring damage, and in some severe cases, can be life threatening. Mites pass easily from one cat to another.

Since several kinds of mites infest cats, your veterinarian must make the diagnosis and prescribe treatment.

Fleas: Fleas are the most common external parasite. If your cat goes outside in the springtime, she probably has fleas, and so will your house in short order. A hungry flea bites its host and prepares the area with its anticoagulant saliva. The flea then siphons up the blood through its proboscis. This causes unbearable itching, and the cat constantly scratches and bites at her skin to relieve it.

Female fleas consume 15 times their body weight in blood daily, so you can see why heavily infested cats can become anemic and sometimes must be transfused. Some cats are allergic to fleas and develop flea-allergy dermatitis. The cat's skin itches, reddens, and develops small sores with scabby crusts. In severe cases, the cat loses patches of hair.

If you turn your cat over and look at her belly, you may see black dots scurrying around. The fur closest to the skin may show tiny black specks of flea fecal matter known as "coal dust." Fleas complete their life cycle by laying eggs on your cat, her bedding, and in carpets. That's why merely shampooing the cat doesn't get rid of the problem.

There's hope of winning the war against fleas, and two recent weapons have been developed to use in the battle—products aimed at interrupting the flea's life cycle. The first are insect-growth regulators (IGR) by the names of Precor (methoprene) or Torus (fenoxycarb). These kill developing fleas. The second is an oral insect-development inhibitor (IDI) called Program (lufenuron), which you mix into the cat's food once a month. It prevents the flea larva from developing normally.

Use these products only as directed. The label <u>must</u> say "safe for cats." If the label doesn't mention cats, do not use the product. Flea products for dogs may kill your Himalayan because they contain a higher level of insecticide than is safe for cats. Remember, cats have poor ability to rid their bodies of toxins.

My tip: To rid your cat and house of fleas, treat not only your cat, but the bedding, carpeting, and outside lawn areas as well. Wash everything your

A flea's bite can transmit microscopic tapeworm larvae to your Himalayan. The larvae migrates to the intestine and develops into a long segmented strand that feeds on the nutrients in your cat's digestive system. Segments of the tapeworm strand break off and are eliminated with the cat's feces. The segments disintegrate and release embryos, which are eaten by flea larvae, beginning the life cycle again.

cat sleeps upon: bedding, rugs, chair cushions, and so forth. Vacuum thoroughly. Outside, rake up debris from under shady bushes and trees. Treat the areas with a flea insecticide, not once but three times at two-week intervals to kill the adult and the new-born fleas.

Ticks: These tiny eight-legged parasites also live on the cat's blood. They burrow into the skin and suck blood. The tick's body swells to many times its original size. Remove ticks promptly. Grasp the tick as close to the skin as possible with large tweezers. Pull the tick straight out, taking care that the head does not remain inside the cat's skin.

Internal parasites

Internal parasites, such as tapeworms and roundworms, live in various locations inside your cat's body.

Tapeworms are long, flat, segmented worms that live in their hosts' intestines and feed off the nutrients passing through the intestines. They are a common parasite in cats, because tapeworms use fleas as an intermediary host. Your cat swallows fleas containing tapeworm larvae during grooming.

Tapeworms usually do not produce symptoms but may, in severe cases, cause weight loss and constant hunger. You may see flat segments of the worm in the cat's feces. Veterinarian-prescribed medication will get rid of these worms.

Roundworms and hookworms live in the intestines and can adversely affect a cat's health. Hookworms can cause anemia due to blood loss, and a common symptom is black, tarry feces. In severe cases, the cat can die from blood loss. Infestation with roundworms is usually not as serious, but can undermine your Himalayan's health and allow other diseases to set in. Both worms are transmitted by infested soil.

Skin Problems

A common sign of skin problems is increased scratching, licking, and grooming. Some skin conditions are caused by parasites, such as flea-allergy dermatitis. Allergic reactions can also cause skin problems.

Ringworm is a common condition in cats, and is caused not by worms but rather a fungus invading the skin's outer layer, causing patches of hair loss. The patches become red and itchy, and develop a crust. Humans can catch ringworm, so provide prompt veterinary treatment.

Feline acne is quite common in cats and usually appears on the face and chin. Openings of the hair follicles become plugged with dried sebum (an oily material secreted by the sebaceous glands) and keratin (a protein substance in hair). When the plug is exposed to oxygen, it changes color and becomes a blackhead. Treat this condition by feeding your cat on plates rather than in bowls and cleansing the affected area with a benzoyl peroxide shampoo recommended by your veterinarian.

Toxoplasmosis

Humans are much more likely to catch diseases from one another than from their pets. However, a few diseases can pass from pet to owner. These are called zoonotic diseases.

Cats can host the toxoplasmosis organism, called *Toxoplasma gondii.* The disease can be transmitted to humans through contact with an infected cat's feces and can cause damage to developing human embryos. Toxoplasmosis also is dangerous to people who have impaired immune systems such as people infected with AIDS, people who have had a course of immunosuppression therapy (given after organ transplant surgery), and those undergoing chemotherapy.

For that reason pregnant women and people with impaired immune systems shouldn't clean litter boxes and should wear gloves when gardening. It's not necessary to give away the cat if you are at risk as toxoplasmosis is transmitted only through direct contact with contaminated feces. If you are concerned, have your veterinarian check the cat for the disease. While cats are a definite transmitter, most cases of toxoplasmosis are acquired by eating undercooked meat.

If you have your cat tested and then keep your Himalayan inside, the chance of you or the cat contracting any zoonotic disease is almost nonexistent.

Abscesses

Abscesses are quite common in cats and are usually caused by animal bites, imbedded foxtails, and other small puncture wounds. Abscesses often go unnoticed since they are small and hide easily under the Himalayan's long fur. The initial injury generally does not bleed much. Abscesses usually appear a few days after the injury as a hot, hard swelling accompanied by pain and sometimes fever. Infection can be life threatening, so it's important to seek veterinary assistance as soon as possible.

Obesity

Since Himalayans tend to be less active than some breeds, their energy requirements are slightly less than, say, an Abyssinian's would be. Because of this, you'll have to watch your Himalayan's weight. Just as with humans, obesity can contribute to health problems such as diabetes, arthritis, and heart disease.

Feel your cat's ribs. An overweight cat's ribs are difficult or impossible to feel. The abdomen may protrude, and fat may hang down below the belly. The cat may also develop bulges of fat on the rump, and the face may become broader.

Always see your veterinarian before putting your cat on a diet. He or she will check to make sure your Himalayan doesn't have other health problems that contribute to her obesity. Never put an obese Himalayan on a strict, extremely low calorie diet. This can cause life-threatening problems.

Obese cats (cats exceeding their optimum body weight by 15 percent), should receive a reduced calorie food. Several kinds and flavors of reduced calorie foods are available.

My tip: To prevent your Himalayan from going on a hunger strike, "wean" the cat slowly from her old food to the new one. Extra play time with your cat's favorite toy also helps your cat stay slim and alert.

The Senior Himalayan

As a Himalayan ages, she becomes less active and more susceptible to certain diseases and illnesses, much like humans do. At first, the signs of aging are not obvious. Perhaps the cat begins to sleep more, becomes less playful, exhibits behavioral changes, and gains or loses weight.

Discuss all changes in behavior with your veterinarian. It's very important to provide an older cat with regular veterinary check-ups, so health problems can be treated before they become life threatening.

Be alert for these symptoms:
• excessive drinking and frequent urination (possible signs of diabetes or kidney problems)
• lumps under the skin (tumors)
• hyperactivity, wakefulness, thirst, diarrhea, increased appetite accompanied by weight loss (hyperthyroidism)
• bad breath, drooling, pain when eating (tooth decay, gingivitis)
• stiff or painful movement (arthritis)
• weight loss (liver or kidney failure)
• lack of appetite, frequent vomiting,

Creampoint Himalayan. The color cream is a genetic dilute of red.

and diarrhea, which may contain blood (pancreatitis)
• difficulty breathing, coughing, shortness of breath, abdominal distention, weight gain, and reduced tolerance to exercise (heart disease).

Personality changes may occur as well. Your cat may be easily irritated and less tolerant of environmental changes. Avoid upsetting the cat by introducing new pets, or subjecting her to rough handling and loud noises.

Your Himalayan also loses some of her youthful agility. Put her litter box, food dishes, and bedding in easily accessible places. Old cats are also more susceptible to heat and cold so keep the house at a consistent, comfortable temperature.

Your cat may spend less time grooming, causing the coat to look greasy or unkempt. Also, obese cats or cats who have arthritis have difficulty grooming themselves.

The senior Himalayan may "forget" her litter box training because of increased urination or bladder or gastrointestinal problems. When the cat begins showing signs of aging, it is a good time to reinforce the cat's early toilet training, to head off problems before they begin.

All of us get old, if we live long enough. Treat the senior Himalayan as you would want to be treated—with gentleness, respect, and love. Your Himalayan has earned it by providing years of companionship.

Euthanasia

Euthanasia (which means "good death" in Latin) is a humane way of ending an animal's life. You may at some point have to consider euthanasia, even if your Himalayan is not old. It's the most difficult decision an animal lover makes. However, consider the cat's quality of life over the pain you'll feel at the cat's death. If your Himalayan is in constant pain and has no chance of recovering, or if the treatment for your cat's disease is not likely to succeed and means great suffering for her, then it's time to let your friend go.

You can remain with your cat, or see your pet afterwards, or not at all. The choice is yours. I prefer to stay with my pets to comfort them, but it's very difficult. The veterinarian can arrange for disposition, or you can handle the arrangements. Pet cemeteries are available in many areas.

If the veterinarian suggests that an autopsy would benefit cat medical research, I suggest you allow him or her to do the procedure. It may make you feel better to know your cat's death benefited feline welfare.

The intensity of your grief may surprise you. Your sorrow may last a few weeks, or much longer. In many areas, pet grief support groups and support hotlines are available to help you through this period. Ask your veterinarian or local humane society. Don't feel silly for mourning. Your pet is not just an animal, but a loved family member. Some people may be insensitive and tell you to simply get another pet (as if cats were as easily replaced as disposable razors). Allow yourself time to mourn before considering another cat. In time, you'll remember the joy your Himalayan brought to your life, rather than the pain you felt when you let your friend go.

Feline First Aid

You can prevent accidents and injuries by making your cat's environment safe (see Cat-Proofing Your Home, page 42). Be prepared for emergencies. Your cat's life can depend upon fast first aid.

Buy the following supplies and keep them handy. Some of these items are useful in emergency situations, others are helpful in nursing the cat after veterinarian treatment. Most can be purchased from a pharmacy or drugstore, but a few you may have to get from your veterinarian or pet supply store.

Keep the supplies in a cardboard box, tool box, or kit marked "feline first aid" (or whatever you like), so you won't have to frantically hunt for them in an emergency. Write your veterinarian's emergency number on the first aid kit as well (check with your veterinarian regarding the after hours procedures and emergency phone numbers).

First aid's objective is to preserve life, alleviate suffering, and prevent aggravation of the injury or condition until you get the cat veterinary assistance. Don't use first aid techniques in place of veterinary treatment. Your priorities in the event of an emergency are to:
• remove the cause of the injury if doing so will not aggravate the problem
• clear the cat's airway and remove constrictions such as collars

Tortiepoint Himalayan. One of the delightful characteristics of Tortoiseshells is the endless variety of patterns.

• resuscitate the cat if she is not breathing or if her heart has stopped
• control bleeding and cover wounds
• treat shock
• then transport the cat to the veterinarian.

Restraint

An injured cat often requires restraint to prevent further injury. The cat may strike out at you when you come to her aid as she may be too frightened to recognize you as a friend. When you approach her, do so cautiously and quietly. If possible, wear thick gloves and a long-sleeved shirt when handling the cat, and bring a thick blanket in which to wrap her. You may need to restrain the cat in order to perform necessary treatment. Use the least force necessary to contain her since rough handling is likely

HOW-TO:
Cardiopulmonary Resuscitation— CPR

Some first aid techniques, such as artificial respiration and cardiac massage, can be hazardous to your cat's health. You can injure your cat with well-meaning but amateur resuscitation attempts. However, since your cat's death is imminent when breathing and heart action stops, you don't have much to lose by at least trying these techniques. Attempt resuscitation when there's no hope of reaching qualified help in time.

Be sure your cat's heart or respiration has really stopped before attempting resuscitation. You can do serious damage if you perform these techniques on an animal whose breathing and heart have *not* stopped.

Be sure to hold your cat's legs above the hock as shown if you are called upon to attempt this resuscitation technique.

Sometimes the breathing can be shallow and the heartbeat weak, but is still present, and therefore should not be assisted. For practice, feel your cat's normal pulse and breathing now. You know your cat is breathing and her heart is beating if she tries to playfully bite you when you try this.

To find the cat's pulse, press your first two fingers against the inside of the upper hind leg, over the large femoral artery. Count the heart beats for at least 60 seconds. A normal, healthy cat's heart should beat between 160 and 240 times per minute. Count either inhalations or exhalations for 60 seconds. In a normal, healthy cat, the breathing should number 20 to 30 respirations per minute.

Artificial Respiration

If your cat is not breathing but her heart is beating, perform artificial respiration. First, take the cat by the hind legs. Hold the cat just above the ankle, one leg in each hand, with the cat's belly facing toward you. Swing the cat forward in front of you, and then back in between your legs. At the end of the swing, give the cat a little jerk. Repeat several times. This drains the fluid out of the lungs, and is also an excellent and safe method to stimulate breathing. This is also a good way to clear the airways of vomit, blood, water, or mucus.

If this technique doesn't work, lay the cat on her side, open her mouth, and pull the tongue forward to open the airway. Press down on the chest with your palm firmly to expel air, and then release to allow the lungs to fill. Repeat about every five seconds.

Mouth-to-Mouth Resuscitation

Mouth-to-mouth resuscitation is another method. Tilt the cat's head up, cover her mouth and nose with your mouth, or hold her mouth closed and blow into her nose. Blow until you see her chest rise. Rest your hand on her chest so you can feel the movement of the chest. Allow the air to be expelled. Repeat.

If your cat's heart has stopped, compress the part of the chest just behind the cat's elbow. Use the thumb on one side and the fingers on the other as a kind of pincher. Compress about twice each second (about 120 times per minute). Stop as soon as the heartbeat can be felt again. You will need to perform artificial respiration as well. Alternate between the two. After five cardiac compressions, perform artificial respiration twice. Develop a rhythm between the two methods and continue until the cat begins to breathe on her own, or until you are too exhausted to continue.

Before attempting mouth-to-mouth, use the swinging method to clear the airways. Then lay your cat on his side, open his mouth and pull the tongue forward. Make sure the airway is clear by looking into your cat's mouth. Then cover your cat's nose completely with your mouth. Blow hard enough to see the chest rise.

Heart Massage

If the cat's heart has stopped, place your thumb on her chest just behind the elbow, and your fingers on the opposite side of the chest cavity. Squeeze gently but firmly about twice every second.

Another method is to lay the cat on a firm surface, and place one hand on top of the chest area, and the other underneath. Compress the chest using both hands.

Observe your cat continuously to see if breathing or heart contractions resume; if they do, stop CPR. If possible, have someone drive you and your cat to the veterinarian's office while you continue rescue efforts.

Medications and Equipment

Activated charcoal tablets
Adhesive tape (½- to 1-inch
  [1.0–2.5 cm] roll)
Antibiotic ointment (ask your veteri-
  narian for purchasing advice)
Antihistamine tablets (ask your vet-
  erinarian for purchasing advice)
Baking soda
Blanket, clean
Cotton balls, cotton batting
Elizabethan collar (available from
  your veterinarian)
Eyedropper
Gauze bandages (1- and 2-inch
  [2.5 and 5 cm] rolls), and dressing
  pads (3 × 3 inch [7.6 × 7.6 cm])
Gloves, leather (for handling injured
  animal)
Hydrogen peroxide (3 percent
  solution)
Ipecac syrup
Kaopectate
Petroleum jelly
Rectal thermometer
Safety pins
Scissors, blunt tipped
Tweezers, blunt
Tongue depressors

to further frighten an already upset cat. Begin with gentle holding and graduate to stronger methods as necessary. Keep calm, and speak softly and reassuringly.

If the cat is frightened and struggling to get away or threatening to scratch you, wrap a towel around her so only her head is sticking out. This allows examination of, or the administration of medication to, the ears, eyes, and mouth. This method keeps the cat from hurting you, and some cats even calm down after being wrapped in a towel. Use a towel large enough to wrap around the cat at least twice.

If you can't towel a cat because of injury or because the veterinarian needs to make an examination, grip the cat's front and rear legs above the hock. Lay the cat down on her side and hold her on the table. This doesn't hurt the cat and prevents her from injuring you.

Before leaving for the veterinarian's office, always call first to let him or her know you are on the way, so he or she can prepare for your arrival. And by all means, drive safely. You won't do your cat any favors by getting into an accident yourself.

Bleeding

To control bleeding, apply direct pressure to the affected area. Make sure whatever caused the injury is not still in the wound before you apply pressure. Place a gauze pad or clean cloth over the wound and press firmly. Hold for several minutes. Tape the gauze pad to the area with adhesive tape. If the blood soaks through the pad, place another on top, but do not remove the first bandage. If the bleeding is heavy, apply firm pressure to the main arteries supplying blood to the area.

Clean minor wounds and lacerations with a solution of baking soda, hydrogen peroxide, or soap and running

Put the bandage directly over the wound and apply firm pressure with your hand to control bleeding.

Sealpoint Himalayan. Notice the contrast in color between the pointed areas and the body.

water, and then treat with an antibiotic ointment. Don't waste time cleaning a wound that's bleeding heavily.

If the bleeding is heavy and doesn't stop with applied pressure, apply a tourniquet to the injured area by tying a piece of gauze tape in a circle, looping it twice over the affected part, and tightening with a tongue depressor or pencil. A handkerchief also works well. Use a tourniquet only for the limbs or tail (never for the head area), and only if the blood loss is becoming critical.

If the cat is bleeding from the mouth, nose, ears, or anus, she may be bleeding internally. Only a veterinarian can assess these injuries. However, a cat who has suffered a fall, has received a sharp blow, or who has been crushed may have internal injuries and show no outward signs. Prompt medical treatment is crucial to the cat's survival.

Shock

Shock occurs when oxygen supplies to the body's tissues decrease due to circulatory collapse. The volume of circulating blood decreases, resulting in lowered blood pressure. Shock can be life threatening.

Shock can occur hours after the initial trauma. A cat in shock appears weak and confused, and may be unconscious or semiconscious. The cat's gums are pale, her breathing rapid, shallow, or weak, and her pulse fast and feeble. The cat's extremities feel cold and her pupils are dilated.

Keep the cat warm. Wrap her in a towel or blanket, and tilt her slightly so her head is lower than her body. This is to keep ample blood flow reaching the brain. If the cat is unconscious, open her mouth and carefully pull her tongue forward to keep the airway open. Do not give the cat anything to drink. Get the cat to the veterinarian as soon as possible.

Fractures

Broken bones are not usually life threatening, unless the vertebral column or skull is involved, or unless the break causes severe bleeding or interferes with breathing or heart action. However, simple breaks can become compound fractures (where the bones break through the skin) or complicated fractures (where the broken bones damage internal organs). To save the cat from additional suffering and further damage, prompt immobilization and veterinary assistance is vital. If the cat has been in an accident, she may have fractures and internal injuries that are not apparent at first glance. Don't attempt to verify a break by feeling the affected area. Do not attempt to push the bones back together.

To keep from aggravating the injuries, secure the cat by wrapping her in a thick, clean blanket or towel. If the cat struggles, bind both the front and rear legs with adhesive tape, wrapped (not too tightly) just above the feet. To transport, pick up the cat gently, supporting both the rump and

Antifreeze is so deadly that a cat may die just from walking through a puddle and then licking her feet.

82

the front legs. If the cat is unconscious or lying on her side, pick her up by sliding one hand under her rump and one hand under her shoulders, keeping her back toward you. Put the cat in a padded box or carrier for her trip to the veterinarian's office.

If help is far away, splint the injury to prevent damage. A roll of newspaper wrapped around the limb will help immobilize it. If you use sticks, use two—one on the inside and one on the outside of the limb. Splinting will only be effective if the splint extends past and immobilizes the joints above and below the affected area. Spine and skull fractures cannot be splinted.

Poisoning

If you suspect your cat has been poisoned (see Hazards, page 40), try to determine what has caused the poisoning, and call the National Animal Poison Control Information Center for advice. The University of Illinois provides this service (there's a fee), and can be reached 24 hours a day, seven days a week by dialing 1-800-548-2423, if you wish to pay for their services by credit card. If you do not have a credit card, dial 1-900-680-0000, and a charge will be added to your phone bill.

Treatment varies, depending upon the poison. Don't try to induce vomiting or neutralize the poison unless instructed to do so, but keep the eyedropper, hydrogen peroxide, Ipecac syrup, and activated charcoal nearby.

Antifreeze poisoning: Indications are staggering and loss of coordination (as if the cat were drunk), panting, convulsions, vomiting, and diarrhea. Other signs include pain, labored breathing, fever, and disorientation.

If you actually see the cat drink the antifreeze, immediately administer one-quarter teaspoon of ipecac syrup to induce vomiting. Don't induce vomiting, however, if the cat is semiconscious or comatose as the cat can choke on her own vomit. Rush her to the veterinarian.

If you suspect antifreeze poisoning but didn't actually see the cat drink any, administer crushed activated charcoal tablets. The charcoal binds the antifreeze and prevents the body from metabolizing it. Then call your veterinarian immediately.

Don't waste time buying charcoal or ipecac syrup after the cat has been poisoned. If you don't have any, rush the cat to the veterinarian.

Breathing Distress

A cat can have breathing difficulties for a number of reasons, including lodged foreign objects, chest wounds, broken ribs, shock, respiratory disorders such as asthma and pneumonia, and heart problems. Acute symptoms include labored breathing (gasping, shallow breathing), pale or blue mucous membranes, unconsciousness, and dilated pupils. Because it is difficult to tell the cause, seek veterinary assistance for the cat as soon as possible. If breathing ceases, the cat must be resuscitated (see resuscitation, page 78).

Choking

Cats, like humans, can get objects lodged in their throats. A choking cat often paws at her face and may make choking sounds. (Don't confuse a real choking crisis with common vomiting. Give the cat a moment to see if she expels the object on her own before attempting intervention.) If the cat continues to choke, open her mouth and pull her tongue forward. Have another person hold her if she is conscious. The cat may try to bite you. Look down her throat with a flashlight. If the obstruction is visible and can be easily reached, remove it with blunt tweezers. However, never try to remove string-like material in this fashion because pulling on the string can cause serious internal damage. Suffocation in cats is unusual; the cat will most likely make it to the veterinarian in time. If the obstruction is too far down the throat to remove, take the cat to the veterinarian to have the obstruction removed.

Caution: If the choking cat is not one you know well, and she has no apparent injuries, do not approach her. Instead, call animal control. Choking can be a sign of rabies.

Heat Stroke

Cats enclosed in small, hot areas (such as in a closed car left in the sun or in an enclosed area like a garage) can develop heat stroke very quickly. The cat pants wildly, foams at the mouth, vomits, and has a very high body temperature. To avoid heat stroke, never leave a cat in the car on a warm day, even for a few minutes; don't leave a cat in a carrier in the sun; and *never* leave a cat in an area without shade.

In case of heat stroke, it's vital to cool the cat down quickly. Immerse the cat in cool water, hose her down, or wrap her in water-soaked towels, and fan her vigorously. Also apply an ice pack to her head. Get the cat to the veterinarian as soon as possible.

Burns

First degree burns are characterized by skin discoloration and singed fur, and second degree burns by blisters and red, mottled skin. Third degree burns are characterized by white or charred skin. Immediately douse the affected area in cool (not ice) water, which minimizes the damage and relieves pain. Sponging the area is also effective. Do not put anything else on the burn (such as butter, which increases the burning sensation), and don't attempt to pop blisters or remove dead skin. Shock is common in burn

A few minutes of cat-proofing your home will go far in preventing emergency situations.

cases. Treat the cat for shock and seek immediate veterinary attention.

Electric Shock

Your Himalayan can be electrocuted if she bites an electric cord. This is a particular concern when the cat is young and playful. If the cat is still in contact with the electrical wire, *do not touch the cat*, because you can be electrocuted. Turn off the power before attempting to help, and remove the cord from the cat's body with a long pole such as a broom handle. *Never use a metal pole or a wet item, and do not stand in water while doing this.*

Symptoms of electric shock include burns on the tongue, mouth, lips and gums, and profuse salivating. In some cases, the electrical shock stops the cat's heart or respiration (see Resuscitation, page 78). Take her to your veterinarian immediately, even if the cat seems all right. Complications can occur hours after the electric shock.

Drowning

Drowning happens rarely, since cats usually avoid water, but they can fall into ponds, pools, and other bodies of water and will drown if they can't find a way to climb out. Kittens have drowned in toilets and other small amounts of water. If you find the cat immediately and the cat isn't breathing, try the resuscitation techniques listed in the HOW-TO section (page 78).

Sexual Behavior

For cats, like all creatures that reproduce sexually, the key to survival is reproduction, and that's why much of feline behavior and social structure is associated with procreation. For example, the tom's habit of spraying to mark his territory is sexual in origin. Since the behavior is dependent on the presence of male sex hormones, neutering usually ends spraying. Sexual hormones motivate both male and female cats from the moment they reach puberty and their reproductive cycles begin.

The Queen's Heat

A breeding female feline is called a *queen*. A Himalayan queen usually goes into her first heat between eight months and one year, although some Himalayan queens can take up to two years.

A queen normally experiences several heat cycles (estrus) in late winter to early spring, and late spring to early summer. However, the queen's seasonal cycles can begin as early as January and can end as late as October in the Northern Hemisphere. (In the Southern Hemisphere the heat cycles are exactly the opposite.) Cats ordinarily do not go into heat October through December.

The day's length regulates the cat's heat cycles. The onset of ovarian follicle growth is caused by increased light stimulation on the hypothalamus. More simply, when the days get longer, the brain tells the body it's time to mate. A day length of 12 to 14 hours seems optimal for bringing queens into heat.

There are exceptions, however. Indoor-only cats, affected by the indoor artificial light, can go into heat any time of year.

Estrus usually lasts for five to eight days, but can go as long as twenty. The heat cycle consists of three stages. First is proestrus, the period before estrus. This stage typically lasts only a day or so. In proestrus, the queen may become more loving to you and to the other humans and animals in the household. She may want to be petted more often, to sit in your lap, or to be near you. It's also possible you won't notice any change in her behavior during this period.

The second stage is estrus proper, when the queen is sexually receptive. When estrus begins, it's usually obvious. The queen meows incessantly, a distinctive sound known as "calling." She rolls on the ground and rubs up against you and the furniture. She may pace back and forth and seem agitated and restless.

She may also assume the mating position called *lordosis*. She crouches low with her back swayed and her tail held to one side, treading with her rear feet while calling repeatedly.

If allowed outside, the queen may disappear for several days, and come home tired, hungry, and most likely pregnant.

Interestrus is the third stage, the period of ovarian and sexual inactivity following estrus. It normally lasts from a number of days to three or four weeks.

Queens can go into heat several times during the yearly cycles if copulation and impregnation do not occur.

Having your normally calm and quiet Himalayan prowling around yowling at the top of her furry little lungs is distracting at best. Spay your cat if you don't intend to breed her. Spaying ends the annoying behavior associated with estrus and is kinder to your Himalayan then allowing her to suffer repeated sexual frustration.

The Tom's Rut

Unneutered adult males (toms) also go through a period of rut that peaks in springtime and declines in fall. It's not clear whether the photocycle governs the tom's sexual cycles like the queen's, or if the tom's rut is triggered by the availability of sexually receptive females, and the pheromones produced by queens in heat.

In general, male cats reach puberty and begin producing androgen (sex hormones) at around nine months. From then on, they spend most of their time seeking receptive females and defending their territory from other males. However, the Himalayan tom is somewhat of a late bloomer, and is not ready to sire until about 18 months.

When a queen goes into estrus, she produces high levels of pheromones with which to attract her mate. Calling also serves as a "come and get it" signal to the male. Toms can perceive these olfactory and auditory signals from far away. This is why neighborhood toms line up on the doorstep when a queen is in heat. The tom shows his sexual readiness by pacing back and forth, spraying urine, licking his penis, and yowling.

Fights for the opportunity to mate may erupt between the competing toms. However, female cats have minds of their own and do not necessarily mate with the fight's winner. Seemingly unimpressed by such macho displays, they sometimes mate with losing males far down on the hierarchy ladder. Queens often mate with more than one male during any given estrus period.

Tom cats are usually not particular about the breed, age, health, appearance, or familial relationship of a mating partner. Himalayan toms will readily mate with, say, Cornish Rex females, regardless of how strange the resulting kittens might look. Toms will mate with their grandmothers, mothers, sisters, and daughters. In humans, that's called incest: in felines, it's inbreeding. Queens are more selective about their choice of a mate, but may still mate with several suitors over the estrus period.

Mating

Before the actual mating occurs, a ritual courting takes place in which the tom cautiously approaches and calls to the subject of his affections. At first, the queen may snarl and strike out at the male. The tom accepts this without taking offense and waits some distance away, watching the female for signs of readiness. An inexperienced tom may try to hurry the female and earns himself swipes from the female's ready claws. The male may make plaintive yowls called "singing," as if to reassure the female of his good intentions.

When the female is ready to copulate she gives an "appeasement cry" to show she is sexually receptive. She assumes the lordotic posture with her tail to one side to allow the tom easier penetration. The tom approaches from behind and mounts the queen, grasping the back of her neck in his teeth. He places his forelegs over her shoulders and straddles her pelvic area. When the position is correct, the tom inserts his penis into the queen's vagina. Actual genital contact lasts only a few seconds and ejaculation is almost immediate.

When the tom ejaculates, the queen lets out a high-pitched scream and turns on the male, seemingly enraged. She may strike at him, hiss, or snarl. This sudden mood swing is unique among domestic animals, and is probably due to the spiny barbs covering the male's penis. The barbs stimulate the female's vagina, and this stimulation triggers a chain of hormonal reactions, producing ovulation.

Felines are "induced ovulators," which means copulation must take place for ovulation to occur. Ovulation ordinarily takes place 24 to 30 hours after copulation. Provoking this hormonal response may be the sole purpose of the penis' barbs, or they may also help the male maintain penetration. No one really knows for sure. Regardless, they are probably responsible for the aggressive reaction of the female following mating, which would certainly be understandable.

Following copulation, the queen rolls on the ground and licks her genitalia. The tom withdraws a short distance away to lick his penis and paws.

Himalayans mating. The male quickly mounts the female and grips the back of her neck with his mouth. Detail: The barbs on the penis are thought to stimulate ovulation.

After an intermission of several minutes to several hours, the mating ritual begins again. Cats can couple many times within the estrus period.

Breeding Your Himalayan

Before Breeding Your Himalayan

It's important to weigh the pros and cons carefully before you decide to breed your Himalayan. To bring new life into the world—whether feline, canine, or human—is an awesome responsibility. It's a decision requiring thought, planning, and experience, and not one to make lightly. Breeding Himalayans (or any purebred breed) is always time-consuming, often frustrating, and, sometimes, heartbreaking. It's also important to understand that, instead of making money breeding Himalayans, you are much more likely to sow thousands more than you reap. For most purebred cat breeders, breeding is a labor of love, a way of life rather than a hobby or a moneymaking venture. Since the price you can charge for the kittens partly depends on the show success of both your cattery and the kittens' sire and queen, you can spend a lot of money attending cat shows and exhibiting, particularly when the shows require travel.

Consider also the domestic animal overpopulation problem. *Very* few litters (*none* might be closer to the truth) are made up of all show- and breeder-quality kittens. All of those pet-quality kitties need good homes, and some of those people buying your adorable pet-quality Himalayans would have instead selected mixed breed domestics from the animal shelters if your kittens were not available. Watching an endless progression of cats and dogs be euthanized because good homes are hard to come by is heartbreaking for the dedicated animal lovers who staff the shelters, and for animal lovers in general. Don't breed your cat without considering the cat population problem and accepting your responsibility to promote conscientious cat ownership.

Feline Genetics

An understanding of the way genes work is vital to your success as a breeder. If you choose to breed your Himalayan, you will need detailed and extensive information on feline genetics. The information here is merely a general overview. See the list of books on page 102 for a few suggestions of appropriate books to read, or ask your veterinarian or breeder for suggestions.

Felines have 19 pairs of chromosomes (38 total). Cats inherit one set of chromosomes from each parent—one set of 19 chromosomes from the mother's egg cell and one set of 19 from the father's sperm cell. These chromosomes are responsible for the determination and transmission of all the hereditary traits such as eye color, hair length, and hair color and pattern.

Sex cells (ova and sperm) are constructed differently. They contain 19 unpaired chromosomes. When a sperm fertilizes an egg, the resulting combined cell then acquires 19 chromosomes from each parent cell, resulting in a total of 38 paired chromosomes.

Sex chromosomes determine the sex of the offspring. Females always have two X chromosomes and males have one X and one Y chromosome

(XX = female, XY = male). If a kitten inherits an X chromosome from her mother and an X from her father, the kitten is female. If, however, he inherits the Y chromosome from the father, the kitten is male.

The chromosomes themselves are made of the building blocks of life—genes. Genes are basically sets of instructions determining the individual cat's characteristics, a blueprint for constructing a cat into a cat instead of into, say, a catfish or some other creature.

Changes in the genetic code create mutations. If the change occurs in a gamete (eggs or sperm), the offspring carries that genetic mutation, and the offspring may show the effect of the mutations. The original form of the gene is called the wildtype, while all the new mutated forms are called alleles.

When both copies of a particular gene are the same (in other words, when the cat receives the same gene from both parents), we say the cat is homozygous for the trait governed by that gene. That trait will be expressed in the cat's physical appearance. If the cat has two different genes governing a particular trait, the cat is called heterozygous for that trait, and the trait may or may not be expressed.

In some cases, the effect of one gene expresses over the effects of another. The expressed gene is dominant, and a gene present but not expressed is recessive. For example, the gene for long hair is a recessive gene. In order for a cat's coat to be long, the cat must get the recessive long hair gene from both parents. If a cat gets the gene for long hair from one parent and short hair from the other, the cat's hair will be short, because short hair is dominant over long hair. Put another way, if the cat is not shorthaired, he cannot have the gene for short hair.

In order for a cat to possess long hair, he must inherit the longhair gene from both parents.

Mendel's Laws

Gregor Mendel (1822–1884), an Austrian monk and naturalist, was the first person to develop a clear understanding of how traits are inherited. Mendel's first law states if two pure (homozygous) animals who possess different genes for one trait are mated together, all of the first-generation offspring will look alike in respect to this trait. For example, if a homozygous shorthaired cat were mated with a homozygous longhair, all the kittens would have short hair because short hair is dominant over long. All of the kittens, however, would carry the recessive gene for long hair, meaning they are all heterozygous for hair length.

Mendel's second law states that if you mate those heterozygous kittens together, both characteristics will show up again in homozygous form. These second-generation kittens, however, do not all look alike and have different combinations of genes. They exhibit three different gene patterns in a ratio of 1:2:1—one homozygous shorthair, two heterozygous shorthairs who carry the gene for long hair, and one homozygous longhair which, of the four, is the only kitten who actually has long hair.

The Pointed Coat Pattern

The Himalayan coat pattern (also known as the Siamese pattern) is caused by a recessive gene that is part of the albino series of alleles. This recessive gene causes a decrease in the amount of pigmentation in the hairs and eyes. Even at the darkest points of the body, the pigmentation is diminished so that, for example, black appears dark sepia-brown, or what is known as seal.

In the Himalayan's color pattern, the body's hairs contain little pigment, but the "points" (the face, tail, feet, and ears) contain more pigment and therefore appear darker. This is because the amount of pigment distributed in the hairs depends on temperature—the cooler the temperature the more pigment is produced. The skin temperature of the body's extremities are a few degrees lower than the rest of the body, and therefore attract more pigmentation. Kittens raised in a cool environment develop darker coats than kittens raised under warmer conditions. As a kitten grows, his coat tends to darken.

Coat Colors

The Himalayan comes in a variety of beautiful pointed colors. The eyes are always vivid blue—the deeper the color the better. Basic solid colors are seal, blue, chocolate, lilac (also called frost), red (also called flame), and cream.

Seal point: The body is an even fawn to cream color, warm in tone, gradually shading into a lighter color on the stomach and chest. The points are deep seal brown, and the nose leather and paw pads are the same color as the points.

Blue point: The body is bluish white and cold in tone, shading to white on the stomach and chest. The points are blue, and the nose leather and paw pads slate blue.

Chocolate point: The body is ivory with no shading. The points are milk-chocolate and warm in tone, and the nose leather and paw pads are cinnamon pink.

Lilac point: The body is glacial white with no shading. The points are frosty gray with a pinkish tone. Nose leather and paw pads are lavender pink.

Red point: The body is creamy white, and the points are deep orange flame to deep red. Nose leather and paw pads are flesh or coral pink.

Cream point: The body is creamy white with no shading. The points are buff cream, and the nose leather and paw pads are flesh pink or salmon coral.

Other Points

The introduction of the agouti gene (A) to the Himalayan results in tabby barring on the head, legs, and tail, and creates the lynx point, tortie point, and tortie lynx point variations.

Lynx point comes in the same basic six colors, but the points are ticked with darker tabby markings. The face mask is clearly lined with dark stripes vertical on the forehead and with the classic "M" on the forehead, horizontal on cheeks and dark spots on whisker pads clearly outlined in dark color edges. Markings are dense, clearly defined and broad, and the legs are evenly barred with bracelets. The tail is also barred. There's no striping or mottling on the body, but consideration is given to shading in older cats, because that is a common occurrence.

Tortie point Himalayans are not barred, like the lynx point, but rather bear unbrindled patches of seal, blue, chocolate, or lilac, and red and/or cream. A blaze of red or cream on the face is desirable. The body color is the same as with the solid colors.

Tortie lynx points come in seal, blue, chocolate, and lilac, and combine the two patterns so the point areas have both tortie patches and tabby markings.

Finding a Queen

When starting a cattery, start with the highest quality queen or queens you can buy. It's important to your success and to the continuation of the Himalayan breed in general to protect the purity and perfection of the Himalayan bloodline. Start with a few high-quality cats—the absolute best you can afford—and dedicate yourself to producing a small number of high-quality kittens.

Ideally, purchase a queen from a well-established and reputable breeder who has a proven track record of producing high-quality kittens. Well-established breeders, however, rarely sell queens to novice breeders. Reputable breeders are extremely selective in placing their breed quality females, and the demand (and price) for show and breed-quality queens is high. "Backyard" and "kitten mill" breeders sell to anyone who pays their price, but their stock is likely to be poor examples of the breed, and may have genetic, health, or behavioral problems as well.

My tip: The best way to obtain a high-quality queen is by going to shows and getting to know breeders. Buying a show-quality altered male and making the show rounds is a good way to accomplish this. The experience you gain from showing and being around breeders and exhibitors is invaluable. Become more knowledgeable by talking with breeders, judges, and veterinarians, by reading about Himalayans and breeding cats, and by joining a Himalayan Cat Club.

After you make initial contacts, try to find a breeder who is willing to become your "mentor," or who is willing to co-own a good-quality queen with you. This method is time-consuming, but your results will be far better and much less frustrating than if you start with mediocre stock.

Don't breed a Himalayan queen until she is at least one year old. If you breed her earlier, she may never achieve her full size, as the nutrients needed for her growth are diverted for reproduction. Before breeding your queen, you should take her for a veterinary examination.

Finding a Stud

Since you probably won't keep a whole (unneutered) male in your cattery, you need to arrange a date for your Himalayan queen. This form of "planned parenthood" is common among breeders, and many established breeders offer stud service.

When you are beginning, it's difficult to ascertain a stud's quality on your own. Your co-owner (if you go that route) can help you. If not, select a champion or grand champion stud, since this is proof the judges have found the cat to be an excellent example.

When selecting a stud, keep in mind the qualities that are important to you. When doing this, study the breed's standard and see where your cat meets the standard and where he could improve. Keep the areas that need improving in mind when you select the stud. Also, consider personality. Personality traits have a genetic base just as color and conformation does. Be sure the stud's vaccinations are current. Combine that with powers of observation, using the same guidelines for selecting a stud as you did when you selected your cat (see page 15).

The Stud Fee

Depending on the stud you pick for your queen, the stud fee could be as low as a few hundred dollars, or it could be much higher for an outstanding, well-known grand champion. The owner sets the fee depending on the merit and value he or she places on the stud's services. The fee usually includes a return visit if the queen does not conceive the first time. It's best to have a written contract spelling out the terms. The agreement should cover the owner's willingness to arrange a second coupling if the mating does not occur. Sometimes a queen rejects the studly male you've selected, seemingly unimpressed by his fine pedigree.

Be sure to keep careful records of the conception date. This is important in determining the arrival date and spotting potential problems later on in the pregnancy.

My tip: After the mating, it's important to keep the queen isolated from other whole males. It is possible for different toms to father kittens within a single litter, and you can end up with some unpedigreed kittens in what you thought would be an all purebred litter.

Make sure the birthing box is placed in a quiet location so your Himalayan will feel safe and comfortable when giving birth.

Pregnancy

Normal gestation is 63 to 66 days but can be as early as 58 days (with greater kitten mortality) or as late as 71 days. About three weeks after conception, a queen's nipples become erect and turn a darker shade of pink. She may develop morning sickness (yes, cats go through it too). The queen's belly will not noticeably swell until after day 30, but the fetuses can be seen by ultrasound as early as day 14.

Nutrition is particularly important during pregnancy. Feed her a food recommended for pregnant cats (see Nutrition, page 58). Don't allow her to overeat. Too much weight gain can make the birth difficult. Avoid medications, vaccinations, or supplements except those recommended by your veterinarian. Keep a pregnant queen away from stressful situations—this is not a good time to get another pet or to rearrange all the furniture.

Preparing for the Birth

During the last two weeks or so, the cat's body looks bumpy and you probably can see and feel the kittens moving. In the last week, her milk will start (you can tell by gently squeezing the nipple), and she may have contractions.

As labor approaches, the queen starts looking for a nesting place. Assemble a birthing box. Make it large enough so the queen can stretch out comfortably on her side and high enough so she can stand, but not so big that's she's lost in it. It should have a lid that's removable so you can peek inside and an entrance that's high enough so the kittens won't tumble out. Line the box with cloth baby diapers, old sheets, or other such disposable bedding. Place an electric heating pad, set at the lowest setting, underneath the bedding, but leave an area unheated so the kittens can move if they become too warm.

The Birth

When the queen reaches the last week of pregnancy, gather the necessary supplies:

- betadine solution
- gauze pads
- hemostatic forceps
- hot water bottle or heating pad
- notepad and pen or pencil
- postage or diet scale (capable of measuring up to two pounds [0.9 kg] in one-ounce [29 g] increments)
- scissors, small, blunt-tipped, unsharpened
- thin rubber gloves
- unwaxed dental floss
- veterinarian's emergency phone number
- wristwatch

On the day of labor, the queen's temperature usually drops a point or two from the standard 102°F (38.9°C). When labor approaches, the queen may seem restless, purr, cry loudly, refuse to eat, lick her vulva, and may pass a bloody discharge. Clip the long hair from the genital area, and from the nipples to allow the kittens easier access. When labor is imminent, the queen will take to her nesting box and stay there. When you know labor is

Weigh each kitten daily. The kittens should gain about 10 grams of weight each day.

approaching, scrub your hands thoroughly, douse the scissors and the forceps in Betadine solution, take a deep breath, and try to remain calm.

The placental "plug" protects the uterus from infection during pregnancy and will be expelled several hours before the delivery. That means the cervix has begun to relax in preparation of delivery. The queen will now experience uterine contractions. Contractions during stage-I labor are slow and rhythmic. During this stage,

These Himalayan kittens were fourteen days old when this picture was taken.

The queen licks her kittens to remove the birthing sac and to stimulate circulation and respiration.

the cervix is softening and opening and the kittens are being moved down to the cervix's opening.

In stage-II labor, the first fetus enters the birth canal and the contractions become more forceful. When the hard (bearing down) contractions begin, the queen usually sits in a crouched position. With each contraction her abdomen heaves, her whiskers arch together in front of her face, and she may cry out and pant. Contractions should be coming at about two- to three-minute intervals and the contractions may come grouped together in twos or threes. Stage-II labor usually lasts about 30 minutes or so but can go longer.

You can clear fluids from the kitten's respiratory passages by slinging.

When the first kitten is born and before the placenta (afterbirth) is delivered, the mother usually removes the membrane called the amniotic sac surrounding the kitten and licks the kitten's face. Sometimes the membrane bursts during the birth process and only remnants remain on the kitten.

The next contractions usually deliver the placenta. There should be one placenta per kitten. Record each birth: time, weight, gender, and when the placenta was delivered. A retained placenta can spell infection and death for the queen. However, *DO NOT* pull on the umbilical cord to dislodge the placenta. If you rip the uterus by yanking on the placenta, the cat will die.

Allow the queen to eat the placentas, because they contain hormones and nutrients. Keep an eye on her, though. An inexperienced queen may not know where the placenta ends and the kitten begins.

About five minutes or so after each birth, clamp the cord with the forceps and, using dull scissors, cut the cord. Leave about one inch (2.5 cm) attached to the kitten. It's a mistake to cut the cord too short. Douse the cord's cut end with Betadine solution to prevent infection. If the end continues to bleed, tie it with a piece of dental floss.

If the queen does not lick away the membrane, gently pinch the sac open and clean it from the kitten's face with a gauze pad. It's important to clean away the mucus and membrane quickly so the kitten can breathe. If the kitten comes out part way and the next contractions do not push him out the rest of the way, you can help by smearing a little dab of petroleum jelly between the kitten and the vaginal wall to help the kitten slide free.

Between each birth the queen rests, cleans and nurses her kitten, and may even leave the box for a time. The interlude may be only fifteen minutes or so, or it could be much longer. The entire litter is usually born in two to six hours, although a rare delivery takes several days.

Pregnancy Problems

If the queen has not produced her first kitten after an hour of hard contractions, or if she partially delivers a kitten and then cannot proceed, call your veterinarian. If she is bleeding bright red blood from her vagina, take her to the veterinarian immediately.

If a kitten is born limp and lifeless, don't give up on him immediately. He may revive if you briskly rub and stimulate him, warm him with a damp washcloth, raise and lower his arms, and blow gently into his mouth. If he feels cool to the touch, place him on a warm water bottle, or hold him in a pail of water heated to 101°F (38.3°C) (with, of course, the kitten's head out of the water).

If the kitten makes choking or gurgling sounds, fluids are present in the airways. "Sling" the kitten by holding him between your hands with the head held between your fingertips. Swing downward gently to force the fluids from the kitten's lungs. Then wipe the kitten's face with a gauze pad.

Kitten Care

It's important for the kittens to nurse as soon as possible. The mother's first milk, colostrum, contains antibodies giving the kittens temporary immunity against diseases. Kittens, blind and deaf at birth, find their mother's nipples by smell and touch. If the kittens try to nurse and then cry, the mother's milk may not have come in. Gently squeeze the nipples to see if milk is produced. If she is dry, call the vet immediately—sometimes the milk can be started with a hormone injection.

Himalayan kittens are born completely white. Their points begin to develop in a few days and darken as

The kittens must be fed every two hours.

they grow. The tiny kittens do nothing but sleep and eat for about the first ten days. Weigh each kitten daily. The kittens should be born weighing about 3.5 ounces (100 g) with a variance of 0.35 ounces (10 g) or so, and should gain about 0.35 ounces (10 g) each day.

Sometimes a queen seems completely disinterested in her kittens. Try putting her scent onto the kittens by rubbing them against the side of her mouth. If she refuses all efforts to make her care for the kittens, try to find a "foster mother" for the kittens by calling your breeder or veterinarian. If you cannot, you will have to place the kittens in an incubator, and feed the kittens by hand every two hours day and night without fail. Use a Catac nurser and kitten formula, both available at pet supply stores. If you can't find a Catac nurser, an eyedropper will also work. Sterilize the nurser in between feedings by immersing it in boiling water for 15 minutes.

At each feeding massage the kittens' anuses and genitals with a warm rag to stimulate urination and defecation. You must do this for the first three weeks as the kittens cannot eliminate on their own.

After about ten days, the kittens' eyes open. It's very important for you to spend time with the developing kittens, handling them and playing with them. Kittens handled at a young age grow up better adjusted and friendlier than kittens that have been ignored or shut away.

Showing Your Himalayan

Cat Organizations

Although cats and humans have had a long history together, it was not until the mid-1800s that people began taking an interest in showing their cats and entering them into competition. At that time, cat organizations and governing bodies were formed to establish and promote pedigreed breeds. The term "cat fancy" has become the common term used to describe the group of people interested in and involved with showing or breeding cats.

Today, cat organizations keep records, register pedigreed cats, monitor cat shows, provide information and training for breeders and judges, communicate with foreign cat associations, feature lectures and publications geared toward the members, and further humanitarian causes. Affiliated clubs generally organize and hold cat shows, rather than the organizations themselves.

The American Cat Association (ACA), formed in 1899, is the oldest United States organization. The Cat Fanciers' Association (CFA) is the largest association in North America and works closely with the Federation Internationale Feline (FIFe), an international organization that oversees European, North American, and Australian cat associations. Canada also has its own association, the Canadian Cat Association (CCA).

The International Cat Association (TICA) originated in 1979 and has additional charters in Argentina, Brazil, Canada, France, Japan, the Philippines, Singapore, and Switzerland.

The National Cat Fanciers' Association (NCFA), formed in 1984, is working to promote public awareness and appreciation of the purebred feline. This organization originally organized because they disagreed with CFA's policy of making the Himalayan part of the Persian breed, and believe that the Himalayan should be promoted as a separate and distinct breed.

The First Cat Shows

The earliest recorded cat show was held in England at the St. Giles Fair, Winchester, in 1598. However, the first cat show as we know them today was held in 1871 at the Crystal Palace in Sydenham, London. The show was staged by Harrison Weir, a noted cat enthusiast of the time who many regard as the father of the cat fancy. The show featured Persians as well as Siamese, the latter disparagingly described as "an unnatural, nightmare kind of cat." The show was such a success that exhibiting pedigreed cats suddenly became all the rage in the United Kingdom.

In the late 1800s, shows in New England featured Maine Coons, an all-American breed. However, after Weir's cat show in England, cat lovers in America caught the cat fancy fever too. The first American all-breed cat show was held in 1895 in New York's Madison Square Garden. Other areas soon followed suit and the cat fancy caught on throughout America.

Today's Shows

The cat fancy has spread throughout the world. Cat shows are held in Canada, Australia, New Zealand, Japan, South Africa, South America, and almost all the European countries. Hundreds of cat shows take place in the United States every year. Even if you don't plan to show, go to at least one for the experience. Cat shows are great places to meet like-minded people and gather valuable information about the Himalayan and cats in general.

How a Cat Show Works

In order to compete in a show, a Himalayan must be pedigreed, vaccinated, healthy, and not declawed. An unpedigreed Himalayan or a part-Himalayan kitten or cat can be shown in the household pet category. Cats must be altered to be shown in this class. In this category, cats are judged on their beauty, character, demeanor, and grooming rather than on a particular breed standard. Many people active in the cat fancy began by showing their cats in the pet category.

Some cat shows are "specialty" shows in which particular breeds, long-hairs or shorthairs, types and conformations are exhibited. Other "all-breed" shows are, as the name says, for all breeds. Some shows also have experimental classes, where new cat breeds can gain exposure and be exhibited without being required to compete.

Cats are registered in one of three show classes: nonchampionship, championship, and alter (called premiership in the CFA). The nonchampionship classes are separated into five divisions: kitten class (cats not under four months but not yet eight months old); any other variety (AOV) class (any pedigreed registered cat or kitten that qualifies for championship or alter competition but does not conform to the standard in color or coat); provisional breed class (breeds not cur-

Exposure to the sun for extended periods can damage the quality and color of the coat. If you'll be showing you cat, keep him inside at all times.

rently accepted for championship status but that have a provisional standard approved); miscellaneous or noncompetitive class (breeds not accepted for provisional breed competition); and the household pet class.

The championship divisions are divided into three classes: open class (unaltered cats of either gender that have not achieved championship status); champion class (cats that have attained championships); and grand champion class (cats that have attained grand championships).

The alter classes are for spayed or neutered cats who would, as whole cats, be eligible for championship status. These classes follow the same eligibility requirements as the championship classes.

Wins made in the championship classes are not transferable to the alter classes. If a champion cat is later altered, he still retains his previously won titles.

In each show, two top awards are bestowed: best of breed (or best of color) to the finest example in each breed present at the show, and best of show to the most beautiful specimen of the entire exhibition.

Showing Your Himalayan

Before taking your cat to his first show, visit a few shows so you can get a feel for the process. Check cat magazines for a list of upcoming shows, or call the cat associations for information (see Useful Information, page 101). Send for a copy of the association's show rules and breed standard. This provides a wealth of information on how to show cats.

Your breeder will have provided a certificate of pedigree and (if the kitten wasn't already registered) a registration form for the association or associations of which he or she is a member. Fill out the form and send it to the proper association, along with the registration fee. If the breeder has already registered the kitten, you'll receive a certificate of ownership. Fill out the transfer of ownership section and mail the certificate (with the transfer fee) to the association. You'll receive a new certificate of ownership.

When the registration form and fee are received by the association, the cat is eligible for entry into that association's shows. If you wish to show in a different association, you have to register him with that association as well.

The closing date for entering is usually a month or more before the show, so allow time for paperwork processing. There's usually limited space available, so enter early. Fill out the entry form correctly and completely and include the proper registration number, all the requested information, and the entry fee. Mail all this to the show's entry clerk. Your breeder may be willing to guide you in the preparation of the paperwork for your first show. After all, the breeder's cattery will gain status if your Himalayan becomes a champion.

If you elect to have someone show your cat for you, name the person on the form. Some exhibitors put down a fellow exhibitor's name they know will be present, so they can leave the show hall to buy snacks (or whatever) without missing out on the judging.

In "show business," your Himalayan's temperament is important, too. Get your cat used to being judged by having friends with whom the cat is not familiar handle and "judge" your cat.

If your Himalayan has never been shown, prepare him for the commotion of the show hall. The cat's mental readiness is just as important as his grooming. Accustom him to being handled by strangers. A cat who bites or scratches the judge won't make a favorable impression.

My tip: Well before the show, have friends come over and pretend to judge the cat. Have them hold up the cat, stretch him out, run a hand through his fur, and wave a feather in front of his nose. Get the cat used to being penned by keeping him caged (inside the house, of course, and for short periods).

Grooming the Show Himalayan

Preparations must begin well in advance if the cat is to make a good impression on the judges. Your Himalayan must look his absolute best. The condition of the cat, in show terms, means not only the physical aspects and the health, but also temperament and grooming.

Most exhibitors spend a great deal of time grooming, bathing, and preening their Himalayans before the show. After a thorough combing, they bathe their cats and use products such as coat conditioners to make the fur soft and manageable. After combing, washing, and blow-drying the coat, and combing again, they backcomb to add body and accentuate the ruff around the neck. They meticulously clean the eyes, ears, and face with cotton balls and swabs. Many exhibitors end by powdering their cats with baby powder or other powder products specifically designed for Himalayan coats. This adds body, absorbs oils, and enhances the show look. Be careful with these, however, as some associations disqualify cats who appear to have excessive powder or chalk. Colored chalk, tints, color rinses and other concealment media can also be cause for disqualification.

Most exhibitors bring a grooming kit with them and groom their cats before entering the ring. For the show Himalayan and his owner, bathing and grooming becomes a way of life.

Attending the Show

When you get to the cat show, the cat is checked in and a cage number assigned. Find your assigned benching cage. Commonly, the perimeter of the show hall is lined with judging rings, while row after row of benching cages crowd the center. The cages are arranged on tables for easy handling.

Sanitize the benching cage with disinfectant before putting the cat inside. Equip the cage with a litter pan, water, food, and a cushion for the cat to sit on. Bring any toys or decorations that will make you and your cat feel at home. Cage decorations range from functional to elaborate. When you've settled in, give your Himalayan a final grooming.

The cat's number will be called over the address system when it's time for the judging. Listen carefully. It's easy to miss the number in all the commotion. Take the cat to the judging ring and place him in the numbered cage. Take a seat in the gallery chairs in front of the judging area.

The judge removes each cat from the cage and examines him briefly. Judging styles vary; some judges keep a running monologue going, others judge in silence. This is the hard part. You've done all you can to prepare, but your Himalayan may decide he doesn't like this judging nonsense and try to leap off the judging table.

After all the cats have been judged, the judge hangs ribbons on the cages of the cats who earn awards, and the cats are removed to their benching cages. When the cats in a particular category are judged, the finals begin, where the cats judged to be the best examples are presented.

This accomplished Himalayan is surrounded by trophies.

Even if your Himalayan doesn't bring home a ribbon, remember he is still your loyal companion, and that the judges' opinions are just that— opinions. In any event, you will have enjoyed a unique experience and developed a better understanding of the cat fancy.

Useful Addresses and Literature

American and Canadian Cat Associations

American Association of Cat Enthusiasts (AACE)
P.O. Box 213
Pine Brook, NJ 07058
(201) 335-6717

American Cat Association (ACA)
8101 Katherine Avenue
Panorama City, CA 91402
(818) 781-5656
(818) 781-5340 (Fax)

American Cat Fanciers' Association (ACFA)
P.O. Box 203
Pt. Lookout, MO 65726
(417) 334-5430

Canadian Cat Association (CCA)
83 Kennedy Road, Unit 1806,
Brampton, Ontario
Canada L6W 3P3

Cat Fanciers' Association (CFA)
1805 Atlantic Avenue
P.O. Box 1005
Manasquan, NJ 08736
(908) 528-9797

Cat Fanciers' Federation (CFF)
9509 Montgomery Road
Cincinnati, OH 45242
(513) 787-9009

National Cat Fanciers' Association (NCFA)
20305 West Burt Road
Brant, Michigan 48614
(517) 585-3179

The International Cat Association (TICA)
P.O. Box 2684
Harlingen, TX 78551
(210) 428-8046

Miscellaneous Organizations and Agencies

American Humane Association
P.O. Box 1266
Denver, CO 80201
(303) 695-0811

American Society for the Prevention of Cruelty to Animals (ASPCA)
424 East 92nd Street
New York, NY 10128
(212) 876-7700

Cornell Feline Health Center
New York State College of Veterinary Medicine
Cornell University
Ithaca, NY 14853

The Delta Society
P.O. Box 1080
Renton, WA 98057
(206) 226-7357

Friends of Animals
P.O. Box 1244
Norwalk, CT 06856
(800) 631-2212 (for low cost spay/neuter program information)

Fund for Animals
200 W. 57th Street
New York, NY 10019
(212) 246-2096

The Humane Society of the United States (HSUS)
2100 L Street N.W.
Washington, DC 20037
(202) 452-1100

Pets Are Wonderful Support (PAWS)
P.O. Box 460489
San Francisco, CA 94146
(415) 241-1460
(Provides pet-related services for people with AIDS)

Robert H. Winn Foundation for Cat Health
1805 Atlantic Avenue
P.O. Box 1005
Manasquan, NJ 08736-1005
(Established by the CFA)

Cat Magazines
Cats
P.O. Box 290037
Port Orange, FL 32129-0037
(904) 788-2770

Cat Fancy
P.O. Box 6050
Mission Viejo, CA 92690
(714) 855-8822

Cat Fancier's Almanac
P.O. Box 1005
Manasquan, NJ 08736-0805
(908) 528-9797

Catnip (newsletter)
Tufts University School of
  Veterinary Medicine
P.O. Box 420014
Palm Coast, FL 32142-0014
(800) 829-0926

Cat World
10 Western Road
Shoreham-By-Sea
West Sussex, BN43 5WD
England

I Love Cats
950 3rd Avenue, 16th Floor
New York, NY 10022-2705
(212) 888-1855

Books for Additional Reading

Behrend, Katrin. *Indoor Cats.*
  Barron's Educational Series,
  Inc., Hauppauge, New York,
  1995.

Behrend, K. and Wegler, M.
  *The Complete Book of Cat
  Care.* Barron's Educational
  Series, Inc., Hauppauge,
  New York, 1991.

Carlson, Delbert G., D.V.M.,
  and Giffin, James M., M.D.
  *Cat Owner's Veterinary
  Handbook.* Howell Book
  House, New York, 1983.

Daly, Carol Himsel, D.V.M.
  Caring for Your Sick Cat.
  Barron's Educational Series,
  Inc., Hauppauge, New York,
  1994.

Frye, Fredric. *First Aid for Your
  Cat.* Barron's Educational
  Series, Inc., Hauppauge,
  New York, 1987.

Helgren, J. Anne. *Abyssinian
  Cats, A Complete Pet
  Owner's Manual.* Barron's
  Educational Series, Inc.,
  Hauppauge, New York, 1995.

Pedersen, Niels C. *Feline
  Husbandry.* American
  Veterinary Publications, Inc.,
  Goleta, California, 1991.

Robinson, Roy. *Genetics for
  Cat Breeders.* Pergamon
  Press, Oxford, 1977.

Viner, Bradley D.V.M. *The Cat
  Care Manual.* Barron's
  Educational Series, Inc.,
  Hauppauge, New York, 1986.

Wright, Michael and Walters,
  Sally, ed. *The Book of the
  Cat.* Summit Books, New
  York, 1980.

Pet Supply Distributors (Mail Order)

Doctors Foster and Smith
2253 Air Park Road
P.O. Box 100
Rhinelander, WI 54501-0100
Phone (800) 826-7206
Fax (800) 776-8872

Master Animal Care
Lake Road
P.O. Box 3333
Mountaintop, PA 18707-0330
Phone (800) 346-0749
Fax (717) 384-2500

Omaha Vaccine Company
P.O. Box 7228
Omaha, NE 68107-9926
Phone (800) 367-4444
Fax (402) 731-9829

R.C. Steele
1989 Transit Way
Box 910
Brockport, NY 14420-0910
Phone (800) 872-3773

Index

Abscesses, 75
Aging, 75–76
Altering, 21, 38
Appearance:
  body, 9–10
  general, 9
  legs and feet, 10
Artificial respiration, 78–79

Backcombing, 53
Bathing, 50–51
Beds, 27
Behavior:
  hunting, 25–26
  language, 22–25
  social, 20–22
Birth, 93–94
  preparations, 92
  supplies, 93
Bleeding, 80–81
Blue point, 90
Body language, 24–25
Breathing distress, 83
  See also: Respiratory
    ailments
Breed:
  origin, 6–8
  standard, 8–12
Breeding, 88–95
  quality, 14
Burns, 83–84

Calciviruses, 65, 67–68
Carbohydrates, 58
Cardiopulmonary resuscitation,
    78–79
Carrier, 27
Cat organizations, 8, 96
Catnip, 63
Chlamydiosis, 65
Chocolate point, 90
Choking, 83
Clubbing, 21

Coat, 10
  care, 49, 52
  colors, 90
  conditioners, 46
  pattern, 90
Cobby body type, 9
Collars, 30
Color, 10
Colorpoint Longhair, 8
Combs, 45
Communication, 22–25
  body language, 24–25
  vocal, 23–24
Cream point, 90

Declawing, 34–35
Dental care, 48–49
Dietary needs, 55–58
Diseases, 65–69, 72–75
Dishes, food and water,
    28–29
Distemper *See:* Feline
    Panleukopenia
Drowning, 84

Ears, 9, 47–48
  ailments, 72
  drops, 71
Electric shock, 84
Environmental hazards, 40–44
Estrus, 85–86
Euthanasia, 76–77
Eyes, 9, 47–48
  ailments, 69, 72
  ointment, 70–71

Fats, 55–56
Fatty acids, essential, 56
Feeding, 61–62
Feline acne, 29, 74
Feline herpes, 67
Feline Immune Deficiency Virus
    (FIV), 66

Feline Infectious Peritonitis
    (FIP), 65–66
Feline leukemia (FeLV),
    65–66
Feline panleukopenia (FPV),
    65, 67
Feline viral rhinotracheitis
    (FVR), 67
Female behavior, 21
First aid, 77–84
  artificial respiration, 78–79
  cardiopulmonary resuscita-
    tion, 78–79
  equipment, 80
Fleas, 54, 73–74
Flehmen response, 23
Food:
  flavors, 61
  guaranteed analysis, 59, 61
  ingredient list, 61
  labels, 59
  nutritional adequacy, 61
  types, 58–59
Fractures, 82

Gender considerations,
    20–21
Genetics, 88–90
Governing Council of the Cat
    Fancy (GCCF), 7
Grooming, 45–54
  backcombing, 53
  for show, 99
Growling, 24

Hair care, 45–47
Hairballs, 54, 68–69
Handling, 31
Hazards:
  household, 42–43
  indoor, 44
  other animals, 40–41
Head, shape, 9

Health care, 63–84
  symptoms, 63
Heat, 85–86
Heat stroke, 83
Hookworms, 74
Housing considerations, 13
Hunting, 25–26

Injections, 70

Jacobson's organ, 23

Kittens:
  and children, 32–33
  care, 95
  homecoming, 31
  nutrition, 58
  selection, 15–16

Language, 22–25
Lilac point, 90
Litter box, 27–28
  problems, 36–38
Longhairs, 7
Lordosis, 85
Lower urinary tract disease,
  58, 68
Lynx point, 90

Male behavior, 20–21
Mating, 86–87
Medications, 80
  administering, 70–71
Mendel, 89–90
Minerals, 56–57
Mites, 72–73

Nail caps, 34–35
Nail care, 47
Neutering, 21, 38
Nutrition, 55–62
  adequacy of foods, 61
  for sick cats, 71
  life stages, 58

Obesity, 75
Ointments, 70
Older cats, nutrition, 58
Ownership considerations, 13–19

breeder, selecting, 17–18
housing, 13
other pets, 13–14
price, 15
quality, 14
sales contract, 16–17

Parasites, 72–74
  fleas, 73
  hookworms, 74
  mites, 72–73
  roundworms, 74
  tapeworms, 74
  ticks, 74
Pattern, 10
Persian, 7
Pet quality, 14
Play, 22
Poisoning, 43, 82–83
Pregnancy, 92
  nutrition, 58
  problems, 95
Price, 15
Protein, 55
Purring, 23

Queens, 85–86
  locating, 91

Rabies, 65, 67
Red point, 90
Respiratory ailments, 67
  See also: Breathing
    distress
Restraint, 77, 80
Rhinotracheitis, 65, 67
Ringworm, 74
Rinses, 46
Roundworms, 74
Rut, 86

Safety, cat-proofing your home,
  42–43
Sales contract, 16–17
Scapegoats, 22
Scratching:
  equipment, 29–30
  problems, 33–34
Seal point, 90

Sexual behavior, 85–87
Shampoos, 46, 50
Shedding, 35
Shock, 81–82
Shopping for a Himalayan,
  13–19
Show quality, 14
Showing, 96–100
  grooming for show, 99
  See also: Breed standard
Siamese, 7
Skin problems, 74
Social behavior, 20–22
  clubbing, 21
  females, 21
  indoor only cats, 21–22
  males, 20–21
  neutered, 21
  other cats, 13–14, 39
  play, 22
  scapegoats, 22
Spaying, 21, 38
Spraying, 23, 37–38
Stain removers, 47
Stud:
  fee, 92
  locating, 91

Tail, 10
Tapeworms, 74
Teeth, 48–49
Temperament, 10–11
Temperature, monitoring, 71
Ticks, 74
Toms, 86
Tortie lynx point, 91
Tortie point, 90–91
Toxoplasmosis, 74–75
Toys, 30
Training, 33, 35
Travel, 14
Treats, 62

Vaccinations, 63, 65
Veterinarian, selecting, 30–31
Vitamins, 56
Vocal communication, 23–24

Water, 57–58